# SUPERSONIC EAGLES

## The Century Series Fighters

Text by
W. D. Becker

## INLAND
## EXPRESSIONS

*Clinton Township, Michigan*

Published by Inland Expressions

Inland Expressions
42211 Garfield Rd. #297
Clinton Township, MI. 48038

www.inlandexpressions.com

First Edition 2012

ISBN-13  978-0-9818157-9-4
ISBN-10  0-9818157-9-0

Printed in the United States of America.

Design by Inland Expressions

# Table of Contents

# Preface

Today, visitors to a variety of museums around the world devoted to the preservation of military aircraft can view a number of aircraft on display belonging to the Century Series fighters. Sitting quietly in their preserved state, these fighter jets betray little of their illustrious past when they once ruled the skies. The Century Series fighters entered service during a period that witnessed significant advances in both aeronautical engineering and electronic technology. As such, this group of aircraft possessed capabilities that were undreamt of just a decade earlier when the first pioneering jets took to the skies.

The aircraft belonging to the Century Series are some of the most remarkable aircraft to have served with the US Air Force. For example, originally designed as a air superiority fighter, the F-100 Super Sabre went on to serve as a nuclear armed fighter bomber in Europe and later undertook the first Wild Weasel missions of the Vietnam War. No less remarkable was the F-106 Delta Dart, which served as an air defense interceptor with the US Air Force for nearly thirty years and was itself derived from the first delta wing jet fighter to enter service, the F-102 Delta Dagger. In an example of the versatility of the Century Series, the F-101 Voodoo, designed as a fighter-bomber and one of the most powerful aircraft of its day, would be produced in tactical reconnaissance and interceptor variants that enjoyed lengthy careers with the USAF.

Perhaps the most unique aircraft belonging to the Century Series was the F-104 Starfighter. Designed as a direct result of the Korean War, the Starfighter would only see limited service with the air force for which it had been designed, but would later emerge as an outstanding export success after being acquired by air forces around the globe. With one exception, all of the Century Series fighters participated in the Vietnam War. It would be during this conflict that the F-105 Thunderchief undertook some of the most dangerous bombing and SAM suppression missions in the history of aerial warfare. Despite earning a reputation for its ruggedness by bringing many of its pilots home even after suffering heavy damage, nearly half of the Thunderchiefs built would be lost during the Vietnam War.

Developed during an era before super computers and composite materials, the designers of the Century Series succeeded in creating aircraft with high-speed performance characteristics not much unlike those of modern aircraft.

# Introduction

On the morning of August 27, 1939, the first flight of a jet aircraft occurred when the German Heinkel He 178 research plane took to the skies. This event, although not fully appreciated at the time by the Nazi leadership, symbolized an important step forward in aviation technology. In 1935, German aircraft designer Ernst Heinkel had become interested in jet propulsion while researching a paper on future engine development. The following year, after receiving a correspondence from Professor Pohl at the University of Göttingen, Heinkel became aware of a young scientist by the name of Hans von Ohain whom was working on a new type of aircraft engine. After meeting von Ohain, Heinkel was impressed enough to hire both him and his assistant. After doing so, Heinkel put them to work at the Marienehe airfield, where they continued developing the jet engine. In September 1937, von Ohain's jet engine came to life for the first time.[1] Such power plants held the promise to allow aircraft to reach speeds unheard of with propeller driven machines.

Interestingly, the maiden flight of the world's first jet aircraft took place just one week prior to the beginning of the Second World War, which began with Hitler's invasion of Poland on September 1, 1939. During this time, Germany's armament factories were hard at work producing conventional weapons for the nation's armed forces, a fact that acted to restrain continued development of the jet fighter in that nation.

Following the successful flight of the He 178, Heinkel managed to schedule a demonstration for the Reich Aviation Ministry to take place in November 1939. Among those attending the demonstration flight were Erhard Milch and Ernst Udet. These two Nazi officials had been instrumental in the establishment of the Luftwaffe along with maturing its capabilities prior to the beginning of World War II. Despite the He 178 performing successfully at the demonstration, the project only received lackluster support from the Aviation Ministry officials. This was largely due to the prevailing perception within the Nazi government that the war was to be of a short duration, therefore, it was felt that such an innovative concept such as the jet aircraft could reach operational service in time to influence the outcome of the war.

While jet engine development was underway in Germany, similar work was also progressing in both Italy and Britain. Outside of Germany, the most promising advancements in jet turbine development took place in Britain. In fact, it was in that nation that the first successful operation of a jet turbine engine had taken place in April 1937. This engine was the creation of Frank Whittle, a Royal Air Force engineer whom had registered a patent for a turbojet engine in 1930. In 1936, Power Jets Ltd. was formed by Whittle and a group of investors to finance the continued development of his engine. Therefore, the 1930s would see Whittle in Britain and von Ohain in Germany working concurrently, but independently, towards making the turbojet a practicality.

The jet age in Britain began on the evening of May 15, 1941, with the first flight of the Gloster E.28/39. As was the case with the He 178, this plane was also a conceptual prototype intended to demonstrate the feasibility of jet-powered flight, and while the design did not directly evolve into an operational aircraft, it provided the basis for subsequent British jet aircraft development.

Shortly after the first flight of the Gloster E.28/39, US Army Air Forces General Henry "Hap" Arnold arranged to have a group of representatives from the USAAF Technical Staff in London to travel to both the Gloster Aircraft Company and Power Jets Ltd. for briefings concerning jet propulsion developments in Britain. These consultations led to the decision to develop a jet-powered aircraft in the United States using a copy of the Whittle engine. Benefiting from its extensive experience in producing turbochargers, the General Electric Corporation, received a contract to build an American version of the Power Jets W.2B engine, designated as the Model I-A.

Meanwhile, a contact to build the airframe of the first US jet was awarded to the Bell Aircraft Corporation, which would build the aircraft at its Buffalo, New York plant under the XP-59A designation. The XP-59A was powered by a pair of GE I-A turbojets, each of which generated 1,250 pounds of thrust. After Bell had finished assembling the XP-59A, it was transported by rail from Buffalo to the Muroc Army Airfield in Southern California where a secret testing program for the aircraft was to take place.[2] On October 1, 1942, with Bell's test pilot Bob Stanley at the controls, XP-59A flew for the first time. Originally nameless, the P-59 was later named the Airacomet.

Although the United States entered the jet age with the Airacomet, early flight tests had proven that the aircraft could barely reach 396 mph, far below the original 500 mph expectation.[3] The fitting of more powerful General Electric Model I-16 (J31) engines into the YP-59A slightly improved this lack of performance. Nonetheless, with a top speed of 409 mph, the YP-59A was still outperformed by contemporary piston-powered aircraft such as the North American P-51 Mustang. Furthermore, flight tests conducted alongside P-47D Thunderbolt and P-38 Lightning fighters revealed that the

A Bell P-59B Airacomet in flight. Despite being jet powered, this aircraft could not outperform many contemporary propeller driven aircraft. (USAF)

Airacomet possessed inferior flight characteristics compared to the two propeller driven aircraft.

Unlike the German He 178 and British Gloster E.28/39, the Airacomet went into production following the USAAF ordering 100 P-59As and 80 P-59Bs. This order, however, was later revised to 20 P-59As and 30 P-59Bs in response to the aircraft's poor performance.[4] Although America's first jet fighter never saw any combat, the P-59 became an invaluable testing and training platform for US aeronautical engineers and airmen during its short career.

Following the first cautious steps into the jet age, the years immediately following the end of World War II, saw exceptional advancements in aviation technology. The rate of progression was such that many designs, once considered highly advanced, became obsolete within a very short period of time. In 1946, the fifty production examples of the P-59 acquired by the USAAF began being retired following the arrival of the more promising Lockheed P-80 Shooting Star. It would be with the P-80 that the

United States had its first true jet fighter.

During the spring of 1943, Bell had decided not to pursue a single engine version of the Airacomet designated as the XP-59B. This decision opened the door to Lockheed receiving a contract from the Army Air Force to develop a fighter powered by a single British de Havilland (Halford H-1) Goblin turbojet engine. Promising to have an aircraft ready to fly within 180 days, Lockheed's chief designer Kelly Johnson and his team went to work following the receipt of a letter of contract from the USAAF on June 24, 1943.

Work on the new jet, designated as the XP-80, progressed quickly with engine tests beginning at Muroc during November 1943. While preparing for its first flight, the XP-80's Goblin engine suffered catastrophic damage when both of the aircraft's engine intake ducts collapsed. As it was not possible to repair the engine, this incident caused the postponement of the first flight until a new engine could arrive from England.

Following the fitting of a replacement engine, the XP-80, dubbed *Lulu Belle*, finally flew at Muroc on January 8, 1944 piloted by Milo Burcham. Beginning with the XP-80A, the H-1 Goblin engine was replaced by the more powerful General Electric I-40 (J33)turbojet. The manufacture of the J33 engine later shifted to the Allison Division of General Motors in November of 1945. Although Lockheed delivered a small number of P-80s prior to the end of the Second World War, the type never saw combat in that conflict. Following the end of war in 1945, and the subsequent military drawdown, the 4,000 Shooting Stars ordered by the USAAF was slashed to just less than 1,000 examples.[5]

In contrast to the P-59 Airacomet, the P-80 Shooting Star outperformed the piston-powered aircraft then in widespread service with the Army Air Force. The Shooting Star was the first USAAF fighter capable of exceeding 500 mph in level flight. The main armament of the P-80 consisted of six .50 caliber machine guns arranged in its nose. Furthermore, up to 2,000 pounds of ordinance could be loaded onto wing-mounted pylons for ground attack missions.

In 1947, the United States Air Force officially became an independent branch of the US Armed Forces, a move that had been campaigned for as far back as 1918. On June 20, 1941, the Department of War had created the Army Air Forces (AAF), which remained a component of the Army but on a level equal to that of its ground forces.[6] Therefore, during World War II, the AAF functioned autonomously without direct interference from either the Army or Navy. Following the transition to full independence, the P, for pursuit, designation was dropped from the Air Force's fighter aircraft and replaced with the F, for fighter, designation. Thus, on June 11, 1948 the P-80 became the F-80 Shooting Star.

Following the F-80 Shooting Star, and before the arrival of the Century Series fighters, no less than four new jet fighters entered service for the Air Force, consisting of the Republic F-84 Thunderjet, North American F-86 Sabre, Northrop F-89 Scorpion, and the Lockheed F-94 Starfire. Of these, the F-86 Sabre would be notable as becoming king of the skies over Korea during a war in which the first jet versus jet combat took place.

The Japanese surrender to the Allies in August 1945 marked the conclusion of history's most destructive war. Soon afterwards, however, came the beginning of another kind of war, one in which the battles between the two major global powers, the United States and the Soviet Union, were fought in proxy conflicts that took place in the far corners of the globe. Although both of these nations had been allied against the Axis during World War II, the opposing political structures of the two powers created a period of uneasy peace following the defeat of Germany and Japan. Lasting for nearly fifty years, this era became known as the Cold War. During this time, the term Western Bloc defined nations that were aligned with the United States. Likewise, the term Eastern Bloc described those nations within the Soviet sphere of influence.

In July of 1945, the United States detonated the world's first atomic bomb at Alamogordo, New Mexico. After using two of these weapons against Japan in August 1945, the war ended with a victory for the Allies. For a few short years, the United States enjoyed a nuclear weapons monopoly. This came to a sudden end on August 29, 1949, when the Soviet Union tested its first atomic bomb.[7]

Assuming, that the Soviets were several years away from building the Bomb, the news of the nuclear test caused quite a shock within the United States. The creation of nuclear weapons ushered in a new perception of warfare as their use could decide the outcome of a war in a matter of hours, rather than weeks, months, or even years. The fact that a single nuclear weapon could obliterate an entire city in just a few seconds required new strategies in warfighting.

During the air war over Europe, Britain and the United States had employed large groups of bomber aircraft to attack Axis targets. Confronted by fighter aircraft flown by highly skilled pilots and large numbers of anti-aircraft batteries, these missions were among the most dangerous of the war. Despite the odds, however, the raids conducted during the Allied bombing effort demonstrated that a large percentage of bombers would break through an enemy's defenses and reach their targets, although at times with survival rates which were unsustainable. However, in an age in which just one bomb could level a large city, the value of sustaining combat operations over a long period during a full-scale war was questionable at best.

As the first generation of jets entered service, the march of progress in aviation technology continued to advance towards achievements, which would have been unimaginable only a few years before. These advancements enabled aeronautical engineers to explore new avenues in their search for the ultimate in both fighter and bomber aircraft designs.

At the beginning of the 1950s, the most advanced aircraft in operational service with the US Air Force was North American's F-86 Sabre. During World War II, engineers at Messerschmitt had discovered that by using swept-back wings the compressibility caused when an aircraft approached the speed of sound could be delayed, thereby allowing for an increase in top speed. Benefiting from this data, along with other intelligence extracted from German testing, the F-86 was the USAF's first swept-wing jet fighter.

The wings were only one of a number of innovations incorporated into the Sabre's design that by 1950, with the arrival of the F-86E, also included an all-flying tail and linked elevators, an adaptation greatly enhancing the aircraft's maneuverability. The benefits of including these design features

A North American F-86A Sabre portrayed with its armament layout. (USAF)

were revealed during flight tests conducted with the Sabre prototype, the XP-86, and Bell's X-1.[8]

The F-86A Sabre had a top speed of 685 mph, and a range of 1,200 miles.[9] Such performance characteristics made the Sabre a remarkable aircraft when it entered operational service. Despite the F-86's ability to break the sound barrier in a shallow dive, the US Air Force would not operate a true supersonic fighter until the arrival of the F-100 Super Sabre.

In February 1949, the 1st Fighter Group based at March Air Force Base, California became the first operational unit to receive the F-86. Just over a year later, on June 25, 1950, communist forces from North Korea invaded South Korea, thus beginning the Korean War. On December 17, 1950, the first aerial kill of a Chinese MiG-15, the Soviet equivalent of the Sabre, was scored by an F-86A belonging to the 336th Fighter Interceptor Squadron.[10]

The Sabre and the MiG-15 had roughly identical performances, with the more heavily armed Russian fighter holding an advantage over the F-86 at higher altitudes. During the Korean War, Sabre pilots dominated the skies with 792 kills for only 78 losses, a kill to loss ratio of 10.1 to 1.[11] This remarkable record was largely due to the American pilots having a higher level of proficiency than their Communist opponents.[12]

As the 1950s began, the United States Air Force faced a tremendous set of challenges, many of which directly led to the development of the Century Series fighter aircraft. As the only opposing nation possessing a nuclear arsenal, the Soviet Union represented a significant threat that could not be underestimated. During this same period, the United States Air Force possessed the only reliable means of delivering nuclear weapons against the Soviet Union and was in the midst of developing a jet powered bomber force to enhance this capability.[13]

While the delivery of nuclear weapons against the Soviet Union was one of its primary duties, the USAF was also responsible for the equally important task of defending the continental United States against attack from the Russian bomber force. To reach their targets in North America, the most logical path for these bombers to follow was over the far northern reaches of Canada. To protect the airspace stretching from Greenland to Alaska was an enormous undertaking, one that would ultimately prove insurmountable. Despite its conclusion, however, the effort placed into protecting these six-million square miles of territory brought about many technological advances in the fields of electronics, missiles, and aviation.

Witnessing Soviet expansion into Europe immediately following the end of the Second World War, the United States and its allies began a massive build up of military forces in Western Europe to deter any further Soviet aggression. The friction between the United States and the Soviet Union created an atmosphere of fierce competition in which both sides attempted to achieve a military advantage over the other. In such a climate, the necessity of heavily investing into military programs garners a much higher state of priority rather than that which exists during a period of peace without a viable enemy threat.

The Century Series fighters represent the second generation of jet fighters developed for the United States Air Force. Collectively, this assemblage of aircraft provided capabilities that were far and above those previously possessed by the Air Force. Designed with the latest technology, much of which was unproven, many of the Century Series fighters would experience protracted and expensive developmental periods.

In retrospect, the rapid progression of aircraft performance following the Second World War is impressive. At the end of the war, North American's P-51 Mustang symbolized the most

The North American P-51D Mustang prototype in flight. The D model was the most produced version of this Second World War era fighter. (USAF)

advanced piston-driven fighter in the Air Force's inventory. The original development of this aircraft began in April 1940 at the request of the British Air Purchasing Commission.[14] Over the next few years, the Mustang was significantly refined and became one of the most respected fighters of the Second World War. In its P-51D form, this aircraft was capable of reaching a top speed of 437 mph when it entered squadron service in 1944. In contrast, just ten years later, another North American product, the F-100 Super Sabre became operational with the US Air Force. With a speed of 864 mph, the Super Sabre was nearly twice as fast as the P-51D.

With one exception, the Century Series fighters were to enjoy lengthy operational careers with the US Air Force. The members of this class also possessed a high level of versatility, as most would be adapted to perform in roles far outside the scope of their original design. The aircraft belonging to the Century Series represent an important milestone in the history of the

United States Air Force as they opened a new era in aerial warfare, one in which it was commonplace for fighter aircraft to operate over vast distances at supersonic speeds. Such capabilities were little more than the work of fiction just a decade earlier.

# Chapter One
## North American F-100 Super Sabre

On February 3, 1949, North American Aviation began development work on a successor to their highly successful F-86 Sabre. This was a privately funded project by North American, which had the goal of designing a fighter capable of reaching supersonic speeds in level flight. Since the first aircraft to exceed the speed of sound, the rocket-powered Bell X-1, had done so less than two years earlier on October 17, 1947, the task of creating a supersonic production fighter was daunting.

Initially dubbed Sabre 45, in reference to the 45-degree angle of its swept wings, engineers at North American began to develop the new fighter by using the F-86 as a starting point. To achieve the supersonic performance they sought, the designers chose the Pratt & Whitney Model JT3 Turbo Wasp engine in early 1949 to power the new fighter. This power plant, which was Pratt & Whitney's first original design, was capable of producing 7,500 pounds of thrust. Furthermore, engineers at Pratt & Whitney also planned to develop an afterburner section for the engine, which would greatly increase its power.[1]

While developing the Sabre 45 design, North American made two proposals to the Air Force concerning enhanced versions of the F-86 Sabre. The first of these offerings took place in August 1950 when an improved version of the F-86D interceptor fitted with 45-degree wings was put forth.[2] This was followed at the beginning of 1951 by another proposed version of the Sabre, this time a day fighter with true supersonic performance. Both of these proposals were ultimately rejected, however, the US Air Force encouraged North American to continue development of its design for a supersonic day fighter.

Meanwhile, the development of the JT3 engine at Pratt & Whitney was also progressing. By 1951, this engine had been redesignated as the J57 and its designers had improved its design to the point that its maximum dry-thrust was increased to 10,000 pounds. While operating in afterburner mode, the J57 was capable of increasing its output by 50 percent to 15,000 pounds of thrust.[3]

As wind tunnel testing continued, designers at North American made the decision that in order to achieve the performance they desired, a completely new design was required. The result of this was Model NA-180, which bore little more than a passing resemblance to the F-86. Feeling that they had a workable design capable of fulfilling the requirement for a supersonic air superiority fighter, North American once again put forth a proposal to the Air Force.

Unlike the previous pair of offerings, this tender was received more favorably by the US Air Force, which ordered two prototypes of the Model NA-180 in November 1951. A few weeks later, on December 7, 1951, this aircraft was designated YF-100 by the Air Force, thus making it the first of the Century Fighters.[4] On February 11, 1952, the USAF issued a letter contract for 23 production aircraft, this being followed in August by a second contract for 250 additional examples.[5]

As the construction of the YF-100 progressed, it received the YF-100A designation, in reference to the numerous design changes made during development. By this time, the aircraft had also become known as the Super Sabre, although it had little in common with its predecessor. Powering the first prototype was the Pratt & Whitney XJ57-P-7 turbojet, which was capable of producing 8,450 pounds of dry thrust, or 13,200 pounds with afterburning.[6] This powerplant produced approximately 15-percent less thrust than the -7 and -39 versions of the J57 that powered production F-100As.

Following its completion at North American's Los Angeles plant, the first YF-100A was transported by road to Edwards Air Force Base where preparations were made for the beginning of the flight test program. On May 25, 1953, North American's chief test pilot George Welch took the Super Sabre into the air for the first time. Despite being flown with an underrated engine, Welch was able to take the first YF-100A to a speed of Mach 1.1 on its maiden flight.

On October 14, 1953, George Welch took the second YF-100A aloft at Edwards on its first flight. While the first prototype was unarmed, the second prototype was fitted with four 20mm cannons and utilized for armament testing. After its inaugural flight, the second prototype proceeded to the Florida Panhandle where it underwent weapons trials at the Eglin Air Force Base.[7]

The first YF-100A (52-5754) is shown deploying its drag chute while landing. (USAF)

Another view of the first YF-100A illustrates the clean lines of the Super Sabre. (USAF)

While piloting the first YF-100A prototype, Lt. Colonel Frank Everest, Jr. set a world speed record on October 29, 1953 when he reached a speed of 755.149 mph over 9.3 mile course at Salton Sea, California. It was on this same date that the first production F-100A embarked on its maiden flight.

The contract issued to North American had stipulated that the Super Sabre must be capable of reaching a speed of Mach 1.3 in level flight. On December 8, 1953, the first production F-100A proved that this specification had been met when it reached a speed of Mach 1.34 at an altitude of 35,000 feet. The US Air Force finally had its first truly supersonic fighter.

The F-100A's primary armament consisted of four M39 20mm cannons, each of which had a magazine containing 200 rounds. Built primarily by the Pontiac Motor Company, the M39 was developed from the German Mauser MG213C cannon.[8] The M39 gun system also armed the A and C models of another Century Series fighter, the F-101 Voodoo. The F-100A's cannons were aimed with the use of an AN/APX-6 radar gunsight, the antenna for which was fitted in the aircraft's nose, just below the upper portion of the engine inlet opening.

The first acceptance by the USAF of a production F-100A for operational inventory took place in September 1954. This aircraft, along with 69 additional examples, featured a shorter fin than the prototypes and began reaching the Tactical Air Command on September 18, 1954. Although the F-100A entered service with the 479th Fighter Day Wing at George AFB, California on September 27, 1954, this unit did not achieve an initial operational capability with the Super Sabre until September of the following year.[9] Early in its career, the F-100 became widely known as the "Hun" within the Air Force, a moniker that followed the aircraft throughout its entire operational career.

During its early months in service, the Super Sabre was involved in a number of crashes. Sadly, such accidents can be a relatively common occurrence when new aircraft types first enter service. To prevent further accidents, the cause of these crashes had to be determined quickly. The first indication of difficulties had come from reports by North American Aviation and Air Force pilots complaining about experiencing stability and control difficulties while flying early production F-100As.

On October 12, 1954, a production F-100A piloted by George Welch broke up over Rosamond Dry Lake while he investigating the reported stability issues. Although Welch managed to eject, he did not survive the accident. An investigation into the crash revealed that the Super Sabre was vulnerable to a phenomenon known as inertia roll coupling. When such an event occurs, the inertia of the aircraft's fuselage overpowers the stability of its flight control surfaces, quickly resulting in a loss of control in all three axes.

Following this and other incidents, the Air Force grounded all operational F-100A Super Sabres on November 10, 1954. Concurrently, North American was limited to manufacturing no more than 24 aircraft a month. Additionally, aircraft coming off the production line were placed into storage to await modifications.[10] As research continued, it was determined that the stability issue stemmed from the reduction in the size of the vertical tail in the production aircraft. Earlier, engineers at North American, feeling that a tall tail was unnecessary, had decided upon this change as part of a weight savings effort. The solution to this problem was a return to a larger tail that was similar in area to those originally fitted to the prototypes and several early production models.[11] Included in the effort to improve the F-100A's stability was a 2-foot extension of its wingspan and an increase in its wing area from 376 square feet to 385.21 square feet.[12]

These design changes were incorporated into North American's production line, with aircraft already produced and awaiting delivery being retrofitted with the larger tail and

A comparison of two F-100As illustrates the differences between the aircraft on the right with the troublesome short tail of the early production models, and that of another Super Sabre with a modified, taller tail. (NASA)

A North American F-100A Super Sabre in flight over a mountainous region. (USAF)

enlarged wings. Furthermore, a program was put in place to replace the tails on aircraft already delivered to the US Air Force, which had banned the use of the F-100As fitted with the smaller tails. In total, seventy Super Sabres built prior to the introduction of the wing and tail design changes received the necessary retrofits.[13]

Aircraft deliveries to the Air Force resumed in April 1955, some two months after the partial lifting of flying and production restrictions. All told, the instability issue had caused about a six-month delay for many F-100A squadrons in reaching their Initial Operational Capability (IOC) with the type.[14] With such problems behind it, however, the Super Sabre began what would become a long and successful career with the US Air Force.

While making a test hop over the Pacific Ocean in a brand new F-100A (S/N 53-1659), on the morning of February 26, 1955, North American test pilot George Smith was forced to eject when his controls jammed following a hydraulic failure. Ejecting from his Super Sabre at an altitude of 6,500 feet and a speed of Mach 1.05, Smith suffered critical injuries. Although seriously injured, George Smith became the first person to survive a supersonic ejection. After a long recovery, Smith was able to return to flying, his ordeal doing much to advance the improvement of ejection systems fitted to supersonic aircraft.

Deliveries of the F-100A to the Air Force concluded in July 1955. In total, North American had built 203 examples of this model of the Super Sabre. The Pratt & Whitney J57-P-7, powered early F-100As coming off the production line, this being replaced beginning with aircraft 167 by the J57-P-39.[15] Even before the first flight of the YF-100 prototype, engineers at North American began design work on an improved version of the aircraft, dubbed the F-100B. This aircraft became so radically different from the F-100 that it was later redesignated the F-107A. Three prototypes of this aircraft were built, the first flying on September 10, 1956.[16] Although a promising design, the F-107A was not ordered into production and the program was terminated in March 1957.

Meanwhile, efforts to improve the F-100A were also underway which would ultimately lead to the development of the F-100C. This included structural strengthening of the wings, which were also fitted with fuel cells to increase the aircraft's internal fuel capacity. To operate effectively in the fighter-bomber role, the F-100C was capable of carrying up to 6,000 pounds of fuel or ordinance on six underwing pylons. The addition of an in-flight refueling probe further enhanced the range and endurance of the F-100C when compared to the earlier model.

The first production F-100C Super Sabre flew on January 17, 1955, and entered service for the US Air Force with the 450th Day Fighter Wing on July 14, 1955.[17] The first F-100Cs built were

Four F-100Cs flying in formation. The C model featured strengthened wings and entered service with the USAF on July 14, 1955. (USAF)

fitted with J57-P-7 engines, with subsequent early production examples receiving the J57-P-39. After 100 examples had been built, subsequent F-100Cs were delivered with the more powerful J57-P-21 engine.[18]

The F-100C had a length of 47 feet, a wingspan of 38 feet 10 inches, and a height of 15 feet 6 inches. The aircraft's overall length increased by 6 feet 11 inches when its chin mounted pitot boom was in its extended position.[19] As was fitted to the F-100A, the C-model was also armed with four fuselage mounted M-39 20mm cannons. With its strengthened wings, the F-100C was capable of a wide range of bombs and unguided rockets on its wing pylons.

One of the key features of the F-100C was its ability to carry extra fuel. The F-100C could carry a pair of 275–gallon drop tanks, which could be supplemented by two additional 200-gallon tanks. However, when the 200-gallon tanks were loaded on the inboard pylons a loss of directional stability was encountered. This later led to the Air Force banning the use of

21

the 200 and 275 gallon tank combination, replacing it with 450-gallon fuel tanks that did not impair the F-100Cs longitudinal stability. Eventual production of the F-100C Super Sabre reached 476 aircraft, of which 451 were built at North American's Inglewood, California facility and 25 were manufactured at their plant at Columbus, Ohio.[20]

The most produced version of the Super Sabre was the F-100D, which first flew on January 24, 1956. The D model featured a Minneapolis-Honeywell autopilot, revised tail surfaces, and inboard landing flaps.[21] Other changes included an increased wing area and provision for a "Buddy" refueling system, which enabled one F-100D to refuel another. This version of the Super Sabre was specifically designed to operate in the fighter-bomber role.

Initial deliveries to the Tactical Air Command (TAC) began in September 1956, and by the end of the year 79 F-100Ds were in the operational inventory. On September 29, 1956, the 405th Fighter Bomber Wing (FBW) at Langley, Virginia became the first unit to become operational with the F-100D.[22] Following the

An F-100D in flight. The D model was the most produced version of the Super Sabre. (USAF)

construction of 1,274 aircraft, production of the D-model ceased in 1959. Of these, 940 of the F-100Ds were built by North American's Inglewood plant while the remaining 334 examples were produced at Columbus.

As guided missile technology improved, the F-100 Super Sabre was fitted with more advanced weapons as they became available. This included the GAR-8 (AIM-9B), an early version of the heat seeking Sidewinder air-to-air missile that was fired using the A4 gunsight.[23] Another addition to the F-100D's arsenal was the GAM-83A (AGM-12B) Bullpup air-to-ground radio guided missile. By late 1959, sixty-five F-100Ds had received modifications to carry the GAM-83A. However, deliveries of the missile fell behind schedule with the first Bullpup equipped F-100D squadron not becoming operational until December 1960.[24]

On September 8, 1955, North American Aviation offered to rebuild an F-100C into a dual place trainer for the Air Force at no cost. Two months later, the Air Force gave it approval for the project after identifying a need for a supersonic trainer to reduce the number of accidents suffered by the F-100.[25] Although its primary purpose was that of a training platform, the two-seat version was to retain the capability of carrying all of the weapons cleared for use with the F-100D. However, it would be equipped with only two 20mm M39 cannons rather than the four fitted to the F-100D. In December 1955, the USAF issued a contract for 259 examples of the two-place aircraft while at the same time reducing their F-100D procurement. This version of the Super Sabre would be designated as the F-100F.

Meanwhile, the Air Force returned a single F-100C (54-1966) to North American to be converted into a two-seat prototype. The modified aircraft, designated as the TF-100C, flew for the first time on August 6, 1956. The first production F-100F, took to the skies seven months later, on March 7, 1957.[26] The addition of a second crew position required the F-100F have a longer

The North American TF-100C (54-1966) is shown on takeoff. This aircraft was a converted F-100C that served as the prototype for the F-100F. (USAF)

fuselage than previous models of the Super Sabre. Without its pitot boom extended, the F-100F measured 52 feet 3 inches in length and had a maximum take off weight of 39,122 pounds.[27] When deliveries of the F-100F concluded in September 1959, North American had produced no less than 339 examples.

The F-100F later served with distinction during the Vietnam War in the Forward Air Controller (FAC) role, while also pioneering SAM suppression tactics during the first Wild Weasel missions. On August 7, 1959, during Operation Julius Caesar, two F-100Fs successfully completed the first flight over the North Pole by jet fighter aircraft.

While in service for the US Air Force, the F-100 Super Sabre filled a variety of roles. Early in its career, it was the premier air-superiority fighter tasked with countering combat aircraft of the Soviet Union. Later, as it evolved into a viable fighter-bomber, the Super Sabre's duties expanded into ground attack. It these roles, it served widely in Europe as part of the Air Force component of the United States' NATO commitment.

Perhaps the most public role that the Super Sabre performed was being an aircraft used by US Air Force Thunderbirds flight demonstration team. In June 1956, after switching from the F-84F Thunderstreak, the Thunderbirds performed their first show using the F-100C. This continued until December 17, 1963 when the team concluded their 690th and last show with the F-100C before switching to another Century Series jet, the F-105B Thunderchief. The Thunderchief was ill suited as a display aircraft, and only performed in six shows before an accident ended its Thunderbirds career. After abandoning the F-105B as its display aircraft, the Thunderbirds transitioned to the F-100D in July 1964. The team continued flying the F-100D until November 30, 1968 when they concluded their 471st show using the F-100D. In keeping with the tradition of utilizing frontline aircraft for their displays, the Thunderbirds then transitioned to the F-4E Phantom II.[28]

Besides the Thunderbirds, the Super Sabre also served with another USAF flight demonstration team, the Skyblazers. As it was based in Europe, this team was less well known in the United States than the more visible Thunderbirds. Formed in 1949, the Skyblazers performed at air shows throughout Europe and northern Africa. The Skyblazers transitioned to the F-100C in mid-1956, and continued to operate the Super Sabre until 1961 when its host, the 36th Tactical Fighter Wing began its transition to the F-105 Thunderchief. The departure of the F-100 also signaled the end of the Skyblazers as the team was inactivated in January 1962.

A more ominous duty performed by the Super Sabre in Europe beginning in the late 1950s and throughout the following decade was that of a nuclear strike fighter. This mission can trace its beginnings back to 1952, when the US Air Force began placing nuclear-armed F-84Gs based in England on alert as part of its NATO commitment. Although the nuclear alert mission was widely referred to as a Quick Reaction Alert, or QRA, to the pilots and crews involved it was known as a Victor Alert.[29]

Capable of delivering a tactical nuclear weapon against a target throughout Eastern Europe, the F-100 represented a threat that military commanders behind the Iron Curtain could not easily ignore.

While assigned to the nuclear mission, each F-100C was equipped to handle a single Mark 7 nuclear weapon. The Mark 7, or Mk-7, weighed 1,600 pounds and was the first true tactical nuclear weapon deployed by the United States.[30] The Mark 7 featured fusing permitting an air or ground burst detonation, and an adjustable yield of between 8 and 61 kilotons. When the F-100D entered service, the Super Sabre's special weapons inventory expanded to include the Mk-28 (B28), Mk-43 (B43), Mk-57 (B57), and Mk-61 (B61) weapons.[31] The F-100D also introduced a 24-hour Victor Alert capability, a feature that the F-100C lacked.[32]

Faced with heavy air defenses and large numbers of enemy jet fighters, aircrews assigned to Victor Alerts in Europe had few illusions concerning their chances of returning safely from a nuclear strike mission. In fact, some of the assigned targets involved distances in which the F-100s would have had insufficient fuel to return to base after delivering their strikes. In such instances, the Super Sabre's pilot would set a course towards a safe area, where he would have bailed out.[33]

There were two primary methods that Victor Alert F-100D pilots were trained to use when delivering their nuclear payloads against a target. The first was the toss-bombing delivery technique. To use this method the pilot of the F-100D approached the target at high speed and minimum altitude prior to entering into what would essentially become a half-Cuban eight at a predetermined distance from the target. As the F-100D ascended, its AN/AJB-1B Low Altitude Bombing System (LABS) automatically released the weapon at a point in the loop that allowed it to follow a ballistic path to the target. After the bomb was released, the pilot of the Super Sabre completed the half-Cuban eight and accelerated away towards a safe distance before detonation.

A second nuclear weapon delivery method was known as the over-the-shoulder technique. This was very similar to the toss tactic, but differed in that the attacking aircraft flew directly over the target before entering into the half-Cuban eight maneuver. Unlike the toss method, the bomb was not released until the aircraft had passed the vertical in the pull-up. After release, the weapon continued upwards, prior to gravity pulling it back down onto the target. In similarity to the toss method, the duration of the bomb's flight before detonation provided the attacker time to escape the effects of its blast.

Realizing that NATO could anticipate the Warsaw Pact targeting their airfields during the opening stages of a war deeply concerned Western military commanders. Since an effective anti-runway campaign by the enemy would effectively neutralize a majority of NATO's fixed wing assets, this was a very real danger. The Zero-Length Launch (ZEL) concept was one solution to minimize the airfield vulnerability issue. This idea involved attaching a booster rocket to a jet fighter which when ignited, would propel the aircraft off a platform and up to a speed sufficient for it to maintain flight. The first of these tests, involving an F-84G Thunderjet, occurred in December 1953.

After concluding a series of successful launches, and less successful landings using an inflatable rubber mat, the US Air Force abandoned the idea for a short time. This time, the F-100D was chosen to validate the concept that a nuclear armed fighter-bomber could be launched using a rocket booster.

Since the F-100 weighed significantly more that the F-84G, a new rocket booster was required. Rocketdyne developed a booster capable of generating 130,000 pounds of thrust. This enabled the launching of an F-100 from a standstill to a speed of

275 mph and 400 feet in altitude by the time the rocket burned out 4 seconds later. After jettisoning the now useless booster, the F-100D would be free to continue its mission.

The first piloted F-100 ZEL test took place on March 26, 1958, when North American Aviation test pilot Al Blackburn was rocketed into the sky. After this flight, nineteen additional manned launches were conducted using the Super Sabre, the last taking place on October 23, 1958.[34] Despite achieving satisfactory results, the concept was abandoned soon afterwards despite 148 F-100Ds receiving ZEL modifications. During the early 1960s, West Germany's Luftwaffe explored this same process using the F-104G Starfighter, which will be related in Chapter 4.

On April 7, 1961, one of the strangest incidents involving the Super Sabre occurred when an F-100A accidently shot down a B-52B (53-0380) Stratofortress over New Mexico. The incident took place when two New Mexico Air National Guard F-100s from the 188th Fighter Interceptor Squadron were conducting mock

An F-100D (56-2947) participating in a Zero-Length Launch (ZEL) test. Note the special (nuclear) weapon shape under the left wing. (USAF)

interceptions with the B-52B, which was assigned to the 95th Bombardment Wing at Biggs AFB, Texas. During one of the engagements, a GAR-8 (AIM-9B) Sidewinder unexpectedly fired from one of the F-100As. Homing on the bomber's engine exhaust, the Sidewinder quickly ate up the distance between the two aircraft and detonated near one of the bomber's engine pods. Losing a wing, the B-52 became uncontrollable and crashed to the ground a few moments later near Mount Taylor, New Mexico. Out of a crew of eight, three were killed in the accident, while the survivors sustained injuries of various degrees. An investigation into the incident concluded that moisture in a missile's firing circuit triggered the launching of a second Sidewinder after first missile had malfunctioned.[35] In the end, no blame was assigned by the Air Force to any of the personnel involved in the accident.

Beginning in the early 1960s, the United States became embroiled in the conflict between North and South Vietnam. Deciding that an overrun of South Vietnam by the North would represent a further expansion of Communism in the region, the United States came to the aid of the South. In May 1962, several F-100s belonging to the Thirteenth Air Force were deployed to Thailand in an effort to prevent Communist forces from overrunning portions of northwest Laos.[36] During 1964, the situation in Southeast Asia had become so precarious that the USAF began basing some of its jet aircraft in South Vietnam. The Super Sabre was involved in this expansion of the war and by the summer of 1964, F-100s belonging to the 615th TFS were operating against Pathet Lao insurgents in northern Laos out of Da Nang, an airbase located on the shores of the South China Sea 400 miles northeast of Saigon.[37]

Although usually employed as a fighter-bomber during the Vietnam War, the Super Sabre often provided top cover for attacking bombers during the early stages of the conflict. In

29

A 31st TFW Super Sabre is directed into its parking spot at Tuy Hoa AB following a close air support mission over South Vietnam. (DI)

retaliation for Viet Cong attacks in the South, Operation Flaming Dart began which would see the F-100 flying top cover for South Vietnamese attack aircraft during the first USAF retaliatory strikes against North Vietnam on February 8, 1965.[38] Ten days later, on February 18, 1965; the first Air Force raids took place against the Viet Cong in South Vietnam. During this attack, F-100s along with B-57 Canberra bombers attacked an enemy concentration near the city of An Khe.

As the air war over Vietnam intensified, the risks for American pilots increased exponentially as the North's air defenses expanded in both scope and sophistication. The increasing danger facing US air power became clear on March 2, 1965, during the opening day of Operation Rolling Thunder, when Captain Hayden J. Lockhart became the first US Air Force pilot taken prisoner during the Vietnam War. This occurred when the F-100 that Lockhart was piloting was brought down over North Vietnam during a raid against an ammunition dump.

Lockhart was imprisoned for nearly eight years prior to his release on February 12, 1973.[39]

While escorting a strike group of four F-105D Thunderchiefs on April 4, 1965, the first aerial engagement of the Vietnam War involving the F-100 took place. As the strike package was nearing its target, the Thanh Hoa Bridge, it was intercepted by four MiG-17s that were operating under ground radar control. Recognizing the danger too late, the escorting fighters were unable to prevent the attacking MiGs from scoring two victories against the bomber force.[40] In return for these losses, an F-100 pilot from the 416th TFS claimed a probable kill on one of the MiG-17s.[41]

One of the lessons learned during the Vietnam War was the need to neutralize an enemy's air defenses to minimize friendly losses during combat operations. During the early months of 1965, the Bendix Corporation proposed installing Radar Homing and Warning (RHAW) equipment into the F-100 Super Sabre. At the time, the Air Force perceived no requirement for such equipment and rejected this offer out of hand.[42] However, as the skies above Vietnam became deadlier for US pilots the Air Force reconsidered this decision.

In August 1965, acting upon a recommendation from an Air Force committee chaired by Brigadier General Dempster, plans were adopted to utilize the two-seat F-100F as a platform to detect and locate enemy SAM radar signals. During their investigation, the committee had reviewed proposals from both Bendix and Applied Technology Inc. (ATI). The head of the project, John Paup, decided to proceed with the offering from ATI. Originally known as Project Ferret, the program was later renamed Project Wild Weasel.[43]

Since the F-100F had two crew stations and a supersonic performance capability it was a logical choice for reconfiguration into a Wild Weasel platform. Originally developed as a training aircraft, an Electronic Warfare Officer (EWO) would now occupy the rear seat of an F-100F modified for the SAM suppression mission. The EWO fought in an invisible form of warfare, as he was responsible for operating the various pieces of electronic equipment installed to detect and locate the enemy SAM threat.

Installed into the F-100Fs modified for the Wild Weasel mission was the Vector IV (APR-25) RHAW system, which provided 360-degree coverage of S, C, and X-band radar signals. Also installed was the IR-133 panoramic scan receiver, which could distinguish between different types of radar signatures, such as SAM, anti-aircraft artillery (AAA), and ground control intercept (GCI). Rounding out the new equipment was the WR-300 (APR-26) launch warning receiver that would warn of an imminent launch of an SA-2 Guideline missile by detecting changes in the targeting radar's signal.[44]

Participation in Wild Weasel operations represented a serious commitment by the crewmembers involved in these highly dangerous missions. To fulfill their mission requirements, aircraft tasked to such operations must act as "bait" to entice an enemy SAM site to reveal their position by targeting them with their radars. Once located, the anti-aircraft installation is vulnerable to attack from either the Wild Weasel aircraft, or other strike fighters tasked to the mission.

Fitted with newly installed radar detection and homing systems, the F-100Fs and their crews began operational training at Eglin Air Force Base in late August 1965. During this period, the personnel involved in the project received instruction on the capabilities, and limitations, of both the enemy's missile systems as well as their own equipment. Following a work up period that lasted three months, the first four F-100Fs configured for Wild Weasel missions arrived at Korat RTAB in northeast Thailand on November 24, 1965. Little more than a week later, on first day of December, the first Wild Weasel mission was conducted.

While conducting a Wild Weasel mission over North Vietnam on December 22, 1965, an F-100F crewed by pilot Captain Allen Lamb and EWO Captain Jack Donovan detected SAM radar emissions originating 95 miles away from a SA-2 site's Fan Song radar. Accompanying the F-100F during this operation were four F-105 Thunderchiefs that would assist in the destruction of any SAM site located by the Wild Weasel aircraft. After closing on the enemy missile site, it was engaged with 2.75-inch rockets fired by the F-100F, while the trailing F-105s did likewise once they were within range. As the strike continued, Captain Lamb spotted the missile site's radar van and silenced it with his 20mm cannons.[45] This mission signified the first successful Wild Weasel mission, and earned Captains Lamb and Donovan the Distinguished Flying Cross.

In March 1966, the F-100F Wild Weasel aircraft received the capability to fire the AGM-45 Shrike Anti-Radiation Missile (ARM). While providing the first steps towards minimizing the

An F-100F belonging to the 20th TFW pictured on June 11, 1966. (USAF)

threat posed by surface to air missiles in Southeast Asia, the F-100F only served as a Wild Weasel in SEA through July 1966. Earlier that year, General Dempster decided to proceed with the development of the F-105F as a dedicated SAM suppression aircraft.[46]

Besides operating in a close support role for combat troops and as a SAM suppression platform, the Super Sabre was also pressed into duty as a Forward Air Controller (FAC) in SEA. These operations, codenamed Commando Sabre but better known by their radio call sign Misty, began in 1967 when a group of volunteers piloting F-100Fs out of Phu Cat Air Base in South Vietnam started flying FAC missions. One of the principal goals for the Misty operations was to disrupt the flow of supplies from North Vietnam into the South along the Ho Chi Minh Trail. As such, Misty F-100Fs operated primarily over North Vietnam and Laos. Pilots assigned to Misty duties were faced with a multitude of threats from the ground, particularly from anti-aircraft guns. In 1969, Misty operations moved to Tuy Hoa, where they remained until the program ended in May of 1970. By that time, seven Misty pilots had been killed in action while another three had been taken prisoner.

During its operational career in SEA, the F-100 Super Sabre was one the hardest worked US fighter types to have served in the Vietnam War. When its involvement in the conflict ended in July of 1971, no less than 238 Super Sabres had been lost, of which 193 were destroyed by enemy action and 45 to operational accidents.[47] In fact, the Super Sabre logged more missions during the air war in Vietnam, than did the 15,000 P-51 Mustangs that flew during the Second World War.[48]

As newer aircraft came into service during the late 1960s, the Super Sabre began to leave front line units, in many cases being reassigned to National Guard units. By this time, the Air Force was deploying the F-4 Phantom II in both the air-superiority and fighter-bomber roles, while the A-7 Corsair II began to take over the close air support mission from the Super Sabre in SEA. In June 1972, the Tactical Air Command retired its last Super Sabre, closing the chapter on the type's service in front line units.

By the late 1970s, the F-100 was also being phased out of National Guard service as more advanced jets became available, with the last Super Sabre squadron standing down in November 1979. After being retired, over 200 Super Sabres, consisting mostly of F-100Ds and a small number of F-100Fs, were converted into QF-100 drones for use in air-to-air pilot training and missile development work. The Super Sabre was one of four Century Series fighters converted into pilotless drones following the end of its service career, the others being the F-102 Delta Dagger, F-104 Starfighter, and the F-106 Delta Dart. During the 1980s, QF-100s were used heavily during live fire exercises, with many being expended by the end of the decade.

Besides serving in the US Air Force, the Super Sabre found its way into the air forces of four other nations around the world. This consisted of the Republic of China (Taiwan), Denmark, France, and Turkey. During the early 1960s, North American

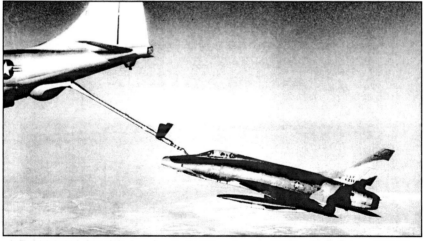

A F-100C (54-2114) belonging to the New Jersey ANG refuels from a KC-97 aerial tanker using the probe-and-drogue method. (USAF)

Aviation had offered an all-weather version of the Super Sabre, the F-100J, to Japan, which later rejected the proposal.[49]

The Republic of China became the sole foreign operator of the F-100A when it took delivery of its first aircraft in 1959. This air force also received four RF-100As, which were the survivors of the six-plane Slick Chick program undertaken by the US Air Force beginning in 1955 to outfit the Super Sabre as a photoreconnaissance platform. Many Taiwanese F-100As were employed in intelligence gathering missions directed at mainland China. Although verifiable details concerning these operations are vague at best, it is widely believed that several aircraft were lost during these missions. In 1984, Taiwan withdrew their last Super Sabres from active service.

France's Armée de l'Air, received its first F-100F Super Sabre on May 1, 1958. In total, 100 aircraft were eventually acquired, consisting of 85 F-100Ds and 15 F-100Fs.[50] During their early years in service, French Super Sabres were assigned to NATO duties. This changed in 1966, when the French left NATO and redeployed its aircraft back onto French soil.

In November 1954, war broke out in the French colony of Algeria, as nationalists began fighting for their nation's independence. During this conflict, French F-100Ds were tasked with bombing missions originating at their bases in France against targets across the Mediterranean in Algeria. Beginning in 1959, EC 1/3 Navarre based at Rheims was one such unit tasked with missions in support of the French effort to quell the insurgent war in the African colony. Since the distance involved prevented the Super Sabres from flying directly back to Rheims after attacking their targets, a stop in the south of France at Istres for refueling was required on the return leg of these missions.[51] In 1962, the war finally ended, with Algeria winning its independence. In 1978, after twenty years of service, the last Armée de l'Air Super Sabre was withdrawn from service.

In July 1959, Denmark became the second European nation to operate the Super Sabre when it took delivery of its first aircraft. By 1961, Denmark had been supplied with a total of 48 F-100Ds and 10 two-seat F-100Fs.[52] Despite losing a large number of aircraft, the Super Sabre remained in service for Denmark until the early 80s when it was finally retired.

Outside of the United States, the largest operator of the Super Sabre was Turkey, which eventually operated up to 206 examples after acquiring the type for the first time in 1958. This number included the F-100C, D, and F models, most of which were received second hand from the United States, while a smaller number were acquired from Denmark. Turkey operated the Super Sabre until 1982, with the type seeing action during the 1974 conflict with Greece concerning Cyprus.

Total production of all Super Sabre models totaled 2,294 aircraft.[53] The type experienced a high accident rate with the US Air Force losing some 889 Super Sabres during its operational career.[54] Today, several examples have been preserved as museum display aircraft in Denmark, France, Germany, the Netherlands, Taiwan, Turkey, the United Kingdom, and the United States.

# Chapter Two
## McDonnell F-101 Voodoo

The origin of the F-101 Voodoo can be traced back to early 1946 when the USAAF's Air Materiel Command (AMC) issued a requirement for a long-range escort fighter embodying a secondary ground attack capability. To meet this specification, the McDonnell Aircraft Corporation commenced working on its Model 36 penetration fighter program. Chosen as project engineer was E. M. "Bud" Flesh, while Dave Lewis was assigned as chief of aerodynamics.[1] McDonnell began working on its Model 36 design on April 1, 1946 and received a Letter of Intent from the USAAF one month later, on 7 May.[2]

Powered by a pair of Westinghouse J34 turbojet engines and required to carry a sizable payload of fuel to meet the specified combat range of 1,500 miles, the proposed design provided a large amount of internal volume. During August 1946, a full-scale mock-up was presented to the USAAF. On February 14, 1947, the USAAF awarded McDonnell a contract for the building and testing of two XP-88 prototypes at a cost of $5.3 million.[3]

In June 1948, to reflect the dropping of the pursuit designation by the US Air Force for its fighter aircraft, the two XP-88 prototypes were redesignated as XF-88s. Two months later, on August 11, 1948, the first XF-88 (46-525) was rolled out at McDonnell's St. Louis, Missouri Plant. This aircraft was subsequently transported to Muroc AFB, California, where it would begin the flight test phase of the program.[4]

On October 20, 1948, piloted by McDonnell's test pilot Robert M. Edholm, the XF-88 took to the air for the first time. Powering the number one XF-88 were a pair of 3,000 pound thrust Westinghouse XJ34-WE-13 axial-flow turbojets.[5] This powerplant arrangement, however, led to the XF-88 being underpowered and thus its top speed of 641 mph in level flight was significantly slower than anticipated. Prior to prototype's first flight, McDonnell's E. M. Flesh approached Westinghouse concerning the possibility of fitting an afterburning section to its J34 engine.[6] Due to ground clearance considerations, however, the afterburner was limited to having a maximum length of 52 inches. Not receiving a positive response from Westinghouse, McDonnell was compelled to proceed with the development of its own afterburner. In this, engineers at McDonnell were successful as they developed an afterburner with a length of 30 inches that boosted the thrust of the XJ34-WE-15 turbojet by 34 percent from 3,600 to 4,825 pounds.[7]

The number one XF-88 (46-0525) Voodoo in flight. The design of this aircraft served as the basis for the development of the F-101. (USAF)

McDonnell's St. Louis Plant bordered Lambert Field, and it was from this location that the second aircraft, the XF-88A, now designated as the Voodoo, flew on its maiden flight on April 26, 1949. On May 12, 1949, while still powered by non-afterburning XJ34-WE-13 engines, Robert Edholm took the number one XF-88 to a speed of Mach 1.18 during a split-S dive from 42,000 feet.[8]

During the summer of 1950, the XF-88A was chosen as the winner of a competition against the Lockheed XF-90A and North American Aviation's YF-93A. Due to changing requirements and budget cuts, however, the US Air Force terminated their long-range penetration fighter program, thus no production aircraft were to be acquired.[9] Following the conclusion of the competition, both Voodoo prototypes returned to St. Louis from Edwards AFB, with the number two aircraft arriving by truck following it suffering damages in a wheels-up landing incident that occurred prior to the beginning of the fly-off trials.

In July 1949, McDonnell was rewarded a contract to modify the number one aircraft to perform studies of supersonic propeller driven flight under the XF-88B designation. This involved the installation of an Allison 2,500 shaft horsepower XT38-A-5 turboprop engine into the nose of the aircraft.[10] Work on this project was delayed, however, following the before mentioned landing accident suffered by the number two aircraft which prompted the use of aircraft number one in the fly-off competition. After these trials were finished, the number one aircraft returned to St. Louis where its conversion into the XF-88B was completed. This aircraft's first flight in its modified form took place on March 14, 1953, thus beginning a lengthy test program that lasted until 1957. During this period, the XF-88B was able to achieve a maximum speed of Mach 1.12 while in a dive on turboprop power alone, as the aircraft's two J34 turbojets were shut down during the test.[11]

Recognizing a requirement for a long-range fighter to escort its B-36 Peacekeepers, the Strategic Air Command drew up a list of requirements for such an aircraft in January 1951. The following month, under the auspices of Weapon System 105A (WS-105A) the Air Force issued General Operational Requirement (GOR) 101 to the military aircraft industry, which specified a May 1, 1951 deadline for the receipt of proposals.

Responding to this request were Lockheed, McDonnell, North American, and Republic. Lockheed proposed variants of its XF-90 and F-94 Starfire, while North American put forth a version of its YF-93. Republic offered three separate proposals, two versions of its F-84F Thunderstreak along with a variant of its F-91 Thunderceptor. Meanwhile, McDonnell offered an improved version of its F-88 Voodoo.[12]

Modifications to the F-88 design included an enlarged fuselage to accommodate two Pratt & Whitney J57 15,000 pound thrust turbojet engines with afterburning, and the fuel required for SAC's stipulated 1,000-mile combat radius. During the development of the design, the vertical tail was increased in size, as were the inlet ducts to allow an adequate flow of air to the more powerful J57-P-13 engines. Meanwhile, the length of the new design increased to 67 feet 5 inches, just over 13 feet longer than the length of the F-88, and the horizontal tail plane was moved to a location near the top of the fin. However, despite the increasing size of the aircraft, its general configuration remained relatively consistent and was designated Model 36W by McDonnell.

The fact that the Voodoo had been the winner of the ill-fated long-range penetration fighter competition held the previous year, clearly gave this aircraft the inside track against its competition. On November 30, 1951, the Air Force redesignated the new version of the Voodoo as the F-101 to reflect the numerous changes made to the basic F-88 design.[13]

On January 3, 1952, McDonnell received a Letter of Intent

from the Air Force approving the further development of the F-101.[14] In July 1952, the first mock-up inspection took place, which was followed by several subsequent reviews during the next twelve months. The Air Force awarded McDonnell an initial production contract for the improved Voodoo on May 28, 1953. As there would be no prototype aircraft built, this contract called for the manufacture of 29 F-101As.[15]

In May 1954, the Air Force placed a production hold order on the F-101A program that postponed mass production until the completion of Category II tests. This move reflected a more deliberate approach by the Air Force in committing to a particular design following the end of the Korean War.[16] During this timeframe, the Air Force had also specified that the F-101A be capable of performing the nuclear strike role in addition to the original long-range escort requirement.

After being assembled as St. Louis, the first F-101A (53-2418) was shipped to Edwards AFB where it first flew on September 29, 1954. During this flight, McDonnell test pilot Robert Little succeeded in taking the F-101A to a speed of Mach 0.9 at 35,000 feet. On 28 October, the Air Force rescinded its production hold

The first F-101A (53-2418) at Edwards Air Force Base, California. (USAF)

order on the program and by the end of the year, it had received three additional preproduction F-101As as Category I flight testing continued.[17]

During flight-testing, two significant deficiencies were identified, these being the Pratt & Whitney J57-P-13 turbojet's vulnerability to compressor stall, and the F-101's tendency to suddenly pitch-up. These problems, along with other minor issues, led to the Air Force placing another restriction on F-101 production in May 1956, while McDonnell continued to work on a remedy for these deficiencies. The compressor stall issue was later corrected by a reworking of the aircraft's internal intake ducts and engine compressor modifications. Satisfied with the active inhibitor installed by McDonnell to address the pitch-up problem, the USAF lifted its production restrictions on November 26, 1956.[18] However, the tendency of the F-101 to suddenly pitch-up without warning was never completely resolved.

Prior to the Air Force accepting its first Voodoo, several changes took place within the program. The scope of the F-101A program was reduced in 1954, when the Strategic Air Command lost interest in fielding the aircraft as a long-range escort fighter. Furthermore, the Tactical Air Command expressed only lukewarm enthusiasm in acquiring a nuclear strike fighter-bomber that was unable to deliver conventional bombs.

On May 2, 1957, the F-101A entered operation with the Strategic Air Command's 27th Strategic Fighter Wing at Bergstrom AFB, Texas. The F-101A's service with SAC was brief, however, with this unit transferring to the Tactical Air Command (TAC) on July 1, 1957 and being redesignated as the 27th Fighter-Bomber Wing (FBW). All F-101As reaching an operational status would go on to serve in three squadrons belonging to TAC's 81st Tactical Fighter Wing (TFW).[19] Production deliveries of the F-101A ended in October 1957, after

A profile view of a F-101A illustrates the type's T-tail configuration and extended afterburner section. (USAF)

McDonnell had built 77 examples. Of these, only 50 reached operational units with preproduction aircraft being assigned to test duties.

Measuring 67 feet 5 inches in length combined with a typical mission gross takeoff weight approaching 50,000 pounds, the F-101A was a very large fighter, in fact, it was nearly 20 feet longer, and 21,000 pounds heavier than the North American F-100A Super Sabre.[20] The Voodoo was the only Century Series fighter to enter service powered by more than one engine. The use of two engines allowed for a higher safety margin to recover the aircraft in the event of mechanical difficulties or combat damage. When the Voodoo entered service, it achieved the best first year safety record of any US Air Force jet fighter.[21] The wings were swept back at an angle of 45-degrees and fitted with boundary layer fences. The aircraft's large flaps were mounted inboard of the ailerons and gave the Voodoo its unique silhouette.

The design of the Voodoo's undercarriage design provided a very wide track of 19-feet 11-inches for its main wheels.[22] Such an arrangement made the aircraft easy to handle on the ground while also allowing for safe high-speed taxiing. Such a design characteristic was beneficial during Quick Reaction Alert (QRA) duties, and during flight operations being conducted in snow and icy conditions.

With its twin J57-P-13 engines each capable of generating 15,000 pounds of thrust in full afterburner, the F-101A Voodoo was one of the most powerful aircraft of its day. This powerplant arrangement provided the aircraft a maximum speed of 1,070 mph, a service ceiling of 50,300 feet, and a 690 nautical mile combat radius.[23] Equipped with an extendable refueling probe located just in front of the windscreen and a refueling boom receptacle on top of its fuselage between the cockpit and the tail, the F-101A could be refueled in flight by either of the two types of aerial tankers in service with the USAF at the time.

The ninth F-101A (53-2426), piloted by Major Adrian Drew, set a world speed record of 1,207.6 mph at Edwards AFB on December 12, 1957. Prior to performing this feat, this aircraft was fitted with two Pratt & Whitney J57-P-55 turbojets and redesignated as the JF-101A.[24] During its record flight, it was

The unique silhouette of the Voodoo is demonstrated by a banking F-101B belonging to the New York Air National Guard. (DI)

given the name *Fire Wall*, which along with a large Tactical Air Command badge was painted on its fuselage just above the intakes.

The F-101A's gun armament consisted of 4 M-39 20mm cannons, which fired through twin ports located on both sides of the aircraft's fuselage just above the nose landing gear. Equipped with 200 rounds of ammunition each, the guns were installed in the fuselage just behind and below the cockpit. To make room for a Tactical Air Navigation (TACAN) receiver, one of the cannons could be removed.

The F-101A was fitted with the MA-7 fire control system that included the MA-2 bombing system. The MA-2 system included a Low Altitude Bombing System (LABS) and a Low Altitude Drogued Delivery (LADD) system for delivery of nuclear weapons.[25] The F-101A was able to carry a single Mk 7, Mk 28, or Mk 43 nuclear weapon on a centerline store. As mentioned earlier, the F-101A could not deliver conventional bombs.

The F-101A's airframe was stressed for 6.33 g, therefore it was unable to perform aerial maneuvers at a gross weight exceeding 37,000 pounds. This made the F-101A unsuitable for tactical fighter-bomber operations with the Tactical Air Command and the USAFE. Beginning with the fifty-first production F-101 built, the airframe was strengthened to allow maneuvers up to 7.33 g as specified in GOR 101. The strengthened version was designated as the F-101C, and was able to operate more effectively at low altitudes. In December 1956, however, the USAF reduced the acquisition of the A and C models to a combined total of 124 aircraft.[26]

The F-101C first flew on August 21, 1957, with deliveries continuing until May 1958 when the last of the 47 F-101Cs built was delivered to the Air Force. In September 1957, the 523rd TFS of the 27th FBW received their first F-101C. By the end of 1958, 17 F-101Cs had been deployed to England where they served in the long-range strike role while based at RAF Bentwaters.[27] During 1966, both the F-101A and F-101C began leaving the active USAF inventory upon their transfer to Air National Guard units.

The range and performance capabilities of the F-101 made it an obvious candidate to perform tactical aerial reconnaissance duties. While being manufactured, two F-101A airframes (54-0149 & 54-0150) received modifications to convert them into prototypes of an unarmed reconnaissance variant of the Voodoo. Following their conversion to WS-105L standards, these two aircraft were redesignated as YRF-101As. The first flight of an YRF-101A took place on June 30, 1955.[28]

The RF-101A was equipped with the same Pratt & Whitney J57-P-13 turbojets that powered the F-101A and C. It also retained the MB-1 autopilot found in those models.[29] The most notable feature of the reconnaissance type was its elongated nose, which made it easily distinguishable from other versions of

A McDonnell RF-101A (54-1516) on the ramp. Note the elongated nose of this reconnaissance version of the Voodoo. (USAF)

47

the Voodoo. The first production RF-101A flew for the first time in June 1956.[30]

The RF-101A was normally equipped with one long focal length Fairchild KA-1 framing camera, three Fairchild KA-2 framing cameras, and a single CAI KA-18 strip camera. Two of the KA-2 cameras were mounted at oblique angles while the other was fixed vertically.[31] Camera control was provided to the pilot by the Simplified Universal Camera Control System (SUCCS). Due to a shortage of camera units, many early RF-101As delivered to the Air Force did not have complete camera packages installed, a situation later rectified as camera units became available.

The RF-101A entered operational service during May 1957, when the 363rd Tactical Reconnaissance Wing (TRW) at Shaw AFB became the first unit to transition to the type. Thirty-five RF-101As were built for the Tactical Air Command before production shifted to the more numerous RF-101C which incorporated the same structural strengthening pioneered in the F-101C. Interestingly, the RF-101C also possessed the capability to deliver tactical nuclear weapons.[32] The first RF-101C flew on July 12, 1957 with 166 examples being built before the final aircraft was delivered to the USAF on March 31, 1959.

In September 1957, the RF-101C entered operational service with the 432nd TRW at Shaw AFB. During 1958, the RF-101C began its first overseas deployment with the United States Air Forces in Europe (USAFE) and the Pacific Air Forces (PACAF). After deploying to Europe, reconnaissance Voodoos were posted to the Laon and Phalsbourg Air Bases in France, and Nouasseur AB in Morocco. Meanwhile, the 40 RF-101A/Cs deployed to the Pacific during 1958, were stationed at Kadena AB, Okinawa and Misawa AB, Japan.[33]

In 1957, four RF-101C pilots from the 363rd TRW succeeded in establishing three new transcontinental speed records during

The McDonnell RF-101C incorporated the structural strengthening of the F-101C, and possessed a nuclear weapons delivery capability. (USAF)

Operation Sun Run. Originating from Ontario International Airport near Los Angeles, this operation involved six RF-101Cs, two of which were spares, two that were to fly one-way to the East Coast, and two that would fly round-trip back to California. The first aircraft took off at 6:59 a.m., November 27, 1957, with the others following at short intervals. After the first refueling was completed over New Mexico, the two spare aircraft flew back to California, landing at March Air Force Base. The remaining RF-101Cs continued eastbound, with Lieutenant Gustav Klatt establishing a new Los Angeles-New York record of 3 hours, 7 minutes, and 43.63 seconds. As the two RF-101Cs assigned the one-way trip were landing at McGuire AFB, the remaining pair continued heading west for March AFB. Upon their arrival, Captain Robert Sweet established a new Los Angeles-New York-Los Angeles record of 6 hours, 46 minutes, and 36.21 seconds, while at the same time setting a New York-Los Angeles record of 3 hours, 36 minutes, and 32.33 seconds.[34]

49

Following the end of Operation Sun Run, reconnaissance Voodoos continued setting records. In December 1957, a RF-101A covered the broad expanses of the Pacific Ocean between Tachikawa AB, Japan and Hickham AFB, Hawaii in just 6 hours and 3 minutes. Later, on April 15, 1959, Captain George A. Edwards set a world speed record of 826.38 mph over a 500km closed course while piloting a RF-101C at Edwards AFB.

Speed records were not the only benchmarks established by Voodoos and its pilots. On September 25, 1958, during Operation Long Leap, an F-101A flew from Carswell AFB, Texas to Bermuda, a distance of 1,896 miles, without refueling.[35] This achievement is regarded as representing the longest flight made by any Century Series fighter not involving aerial refueling.

The RF-101C remained the Air Force's primary tactical reconnaissance aircraft until the arrival of the RF-4C Phantom II in May 1964. During this period, the RF-101C Voodoo was involved in numerous missions over hostile territory in both the Caribbean and Southeast Asia. Perhaps the most critical of these missions were the ones performed in October 1962 during the Cuban Missile Crisis, an event that placed the United States and the Soviet Union just one-step away from nuclear war.

On October 14, 1962, a high-flying U-2E spy plane captured images providing irrefutable evidence that the Soviet Union was in the process of placing nuclear-armed ballistic missiles on the island of Cuba.[36] Three years previously, a nationalist uprising had resulted in the overthrow of the Cuban dictator Fulgencio Batista. Following this, the leader of the revolt, Fidel Castro, began a socialist transformation of Cuba's government. The formation of a communist state just 90 miles off the shores of the United States was a situation unacceptable to many Americans. The further discovery of Soviet ballistic missiles on Cuba possessing the capability of striking any target throughout much of North America quickly led to the beginning of the Cuban

Missile Crisis.[37]

Following the beginning of the crisis, military planners at the Pentagon began drafting plans for an air campaign to destroy the Soviet missiles, followed by an invasion of Cuba itself. Such plans required a highly accurate appraisal of the military situation on the island so that enemy forces could be located and targeted. To obtain such intelligence, a series of low-level tactical reconnaissance missions were performed by USAF RF-101C Voodoos and US Navy & Marine Corps RF-8A Crusaders.[38]

The first RF-101C missions over Cuba took place on October 23, 1962 when aircraft from the 363rd TRW based at Shaw AFB, South Carolina overflew the Caribbean nation.[39] While the high-flying U-2 spy plane flights produced a highly accurate assessment of Cuba on a strategic level, it would be the Voodoos and Crusaders that provided an insight into the positioning and status of individual enemy military units and facilities located around the island nation. By October 26, 1962, these low-level flights had identified no less than 1,397 separate targets in Cuba for US planners.[40]

The Lockheed U-2 and the McDonnell RF-101C used dissimilar methods in their effort to avoid destruction by an enemy's air-defense system. Capable of operating at altitudes in excess of 70,000 feet, the U-2 was virtually immune to interception by contemporary jet interceptors. It was, however, vulnerable to the Soviet SA-2 Guideline surface-to-air missile, a weakness demonstrated during the shooting down of Francis Gary Powers in a U-2C over the Soviet Union on May 1, 1960. On October 27, 1962, the SA-2 scored another victory against the high-flying spy plane when a U-2 was brought down over Cuba. This occurred during the height of the Cuban Missile Crisis and resulted in the death of the U-2's pilot, Major Rudolf Anderson, Jr.

Unlike the high altitude U-2, the RF-101C relied upon its

ability to fly at high speeds at low altitude to avoid being engaged by enemy air defenses. During these dangerous missions, the RF-101C's cameras captured high-resolution images of objects on the ground that provided photo analysts with a means to base an assessment of the current strength and disposition of military forces in Cuba.

On October 28, 1962, Soviet Premier Nikita Khrushchev announced that the offensive missiles in Cuba would be withdrawn. The following day, a RF-101 returned from an over flight of Cuba with evidence that the Soviet nuclear missile bases were indeed being dismantled.[41] Following these events, the crisis came to an abrupt, but peaceful, conclusion with no major hostilities having broken out between the Superpowers.

The RF-101C would see its heaviest use in the skies above South East Asia (SEA). During the early years of this conflict, the RF-101C bore the brunt of tactical aerial reconnaissance duties as the United States increased its involvement in the Vietnam War. In October 1961, 4 RF-101Cs belonging to the 15th Tactical Reconnaissance Squadron based at Kadena AB, Okinawa deployed to Tan Son Nhut AB, South Vietnam. These aircraft originally arrived in South Vietnam under the pretense that they were to take part in an air show. Following the air show's cancellation, however, the RF-101Cs remained at Tan Son Nhut to begin flying photo-intelligence missions over South Vietnam and Laos during Project Pipe Stem.[42]

During same timeframe that RF-101Cs were arriving in South Vietnam to begin Pipe Stem operations, Thailand approved a request by the United States to station four RF-101Cs at Don Muang Airport to perform similar reconnaissance flights over South Vietnam and Laos. Drawn from the 45th Tactical Reconnaissance Squadron, the four RF-101Cs arrived at Don Muang on November 7, 1961 to begin Project Able Mable.[43]

As the situation in SEA continued to deteriorate during the

An RF-101 is prepared for a photoreconnaissance mission while deployed to Southeast Asia. Note the Fairchild C-123 Provider overhead. (USAF)

early 1960s, the USAF became increasingly involved in the struggle to contain the spread of communism in the region. During August 1964, the USAF bolstered its forces in the region with the additional deployment of 6 RF-101C Voodoos, 36 B-57 tactical bombers, 8 F-100 Super Sabres, and 12 F-102 Delta Daggers to bases in South Vietnam.[44]

Following a Viet Cong attack on a US Army compound at Pleiku on February 7, 1965, a contingency plan to attack targets in North Vietnam went into effect. The following morning, a single RF-101C acting as a weather reconnaissance platform supported a strike against the Chap Le Barracks at Vinh Linh by VNAF A-1 Skyraiders, while two additional RF-101Cs provided post-strike reconnaissance of the target.[45] As the number of bombing missions in the North increased, so did the requirement for photographic intelligence. This prompted the deployment of additional Voodoo reconnaissance assets into the region, operating primarily out of bases in Thailand. So critical was the need for tactical intelligence that by the closing months of 1967 the Tactical Air Command had assigned all but one of its active RF-101C squadrons to Southeast Asia.

On June 21, 1967, a RF-101C was shot down by a SAM 40 miles southwest of Hoa Binh. Although the pilot was subsequently rescued, the incident underscored the increasing danger facing Voodoo pilots over the North. Another RF-101C was brought down by missile fire on August 1, 1967, despite the fact that this aircraft was carrying an ALQ-51 deception jammer. Already suspecting that the ALQ-51 was ineffective against the North's radars, the Seventh Air Force withdrew them from use. The Seventh Air Force also mandated that RF-101Cs were to carry two ALQ-71 jamming pods and fly in pairs on missions over North Vietnam. The ALQ-71 pods, however, represented such a performance penalty for the RF-101C that a fighter escort was required on many of their missions for protection against enemy fighters.[46]

With its high-speed performance at low altitude, the RF-101C Voodoo was able to outrun any North Vietnamese MiG-17 fighter attempting to intercept it. However, the introduction of the MiG-21 into the NVAF during 1966 represented a clear danger to the RF-101C. This Soviet-built aircraft was capable of reaching speeds in excess of Mach 2 and was therefore able to catch the Voodoo under favorable conditions. In September 1967, this proved to be the case when a RF-101C was brought down by a MiG-21, after which Voodoo operations over North Vietnam were curtailed by the Seventh Air Force.

Following being replaced by the RF-4C Phantom II in reconnaissance missions over North Vietnam, the RF-101C soldiered on providing photographic support missions over South Vietnam and Laos. Beginning in early 1969, the Air Force began transferring the RF-101C to Air National Guard (ANG) units as the type was retired from front line squadrons.[47] In November 1970, the last RF-101C departed SEA, and during the following year, the last active duty RF-101C Voodoo was transferred to the Air National Guard. During the war in Vietnam, 33 RF-101Cs were lost to enemy action, while another 6 aircraft were destroyed in operational accidents.[48]

Besides the RF-101C, the ANG operated three other versions of reconnaissance Voodoos, one of which, the RF-101B, will be described later. Following their retirement from USAFE units, 29 F-101As and 32 F-101Cs were converted into reconnaissance aircraft during 1965 and redesignated as RF-101Gs and RF-101Hs respectively. These conversions were completed by the Lockheed Aircraft Service Company at Ontario, California.[49] During reconstruction, the aircraft's original armament was removed to make room for a camera pallet, while the radar was likewise deleted to allow the mounting of a forward-looking camera inside of a revised nose cone. Lacking the elongated nose sections common with the RF-101A/Cs, the RF-101G/H models were easily distinguishable from previous reconnaissance versions of the Voodoo by their shorter and broader noses. The RF-101G remained in service until 1972 when the type was withdrawn from service following the Arkansas ANG's transition to the RF-101C. In turn, RF-101H/RF-101Cs remained active with the ANG throughout the 1970s, prior to their retirement in 1979.

Beginning in November 1959, as part of a project named Operation Boom Town, the United States began transferring a small number of RF-101As to Taiwan to serve with the Chinese Nationalist Air Force. In total, eight RF-101As were delivered to Taiwan under this program, which put them to use flying intelligence gathering missions over mainland China.[50] As is the case with the four RF-100A Super Sabres operated by Taiwan, the details of RF-101A operations are also vague at best. It is certain, however, that some of these missions were not entirely successful, as Taiwan has admitted to losing three RF-101As to enemy fire. During the late 1970s, the Chinese Nationalist Air Force retired its last remaining RF-101As.

During 1952, McDonnell proposed the development of an all-weather interceptor version of the F-101, but the Air Force rejected this due to cost considerations. However, difficulties experienced by Convair during the development of USAF's "Ultimate Interceptor" program had led to the acquisition of the F-102A as an interim interceptor pending the delivery of the more capable F-102B (F-106A). In 1953, just one year after the United States had tested the world's first hydrogen bomb, the Soviet Union detonated their first such device. This, along with continuing delays with the F-102B, prompted the USAF's Air Defense Command (ADC) to insist upon the acquisition of an all-weather long-range interceptor pending the arrival of the improved interceptor. Consequently, during 1953, the Air Force Council invited the aircraft industry to enter into competition for an interceptor to fill the performance gap between the subsonic F-89 Scorpion and the F-106A.[51]

The USAF received three proposals to meet its interceptor requirements. Northrop proposed an advanced version of its F-89 Scorpion. North American, meanwhile, put forward an interceptor based upon their F-100 Super Sabre. Lastly, McDonnell submitted an interceptor variant of the F-101 Voodoo. In June 1954, the Air Defense Command chose McDonnell's proposal as being the best choice of the three designs submitted. In March 1955, the USAF issued a letter contract to McDonnell for the acquisition of 28 interceptors. This was followed by the issuance of a formal contract on July 12, 1955 that increased the total acquisition for the 1956 fiscal year to 96 aircraft. During this timeframe, the new interceptor was given the F-101B designation.[52]

While the overall dimensions of the F-101B remained identical to the previous F-101A/C models, the B model incorporated a

A McDonnell F-101B (58-0312) interceptor belonging to the 18th FIS, Grand Forks AFB, North Dakota. (USAF)

second crewmember to operate the aircraft's radar systems. Despite the dimensional similarities, however, the design of the forward fuselage differed from the A and C models in order to accommodate the second cockpit, and the aircraft's electronic and weapon systems.[53] Since the F-101B weighed more than previous models of the Voodoo, it was fitted with a heavier undercarriage and larger tires.

The addition of a second crewmember limited the internal fuel capacity of the F-101B to 2,053 gallons compared to C model's 2,250 gallons. The F-101B was powered by a pair of Pratt & Whitney J-57-P-55 turbojets. Each of these engines was capable of generating 16,900 pounds of thrust while in afterburning, making them significantly more powerful than those installed in the F-101A/C models.[54] These engines were fitted with long afterburner sections, which when combined with its two-place cockpit gave the B model a distinctive appearance when compared to other versions of the Voodoo.

The first flight of the interceptor version of the Voodoo

57

occurred on March 27, 1957 when the NF-101B (56-232) took to the air at Lambert Field.  The single NF-101B was destined to become a permanent test aircraft.  As was common with aircraft belonging to the Century Series, the development of the F-101B took longer than anticipated with its first flight occurring eighteen months later than had been originally planned. McDonnell would eventually produce 479 production examples of the F-101B before delivering the final aircraft in March 1964, making the B model the most common Voodoo variant built.

The F-101B underwent a lengthy testing program that began with Category I testing at Edwards AFB during March 1957, and concluded with the end of Category III testing at Otis AFB on March 15, 1959.  During this period, two major issues were uncovered.  The first was the poor design of the radar observer's cockpit, for which little could be done without a major redesign. The second, was the lack of sophistication on the part of the aircraft's MG-13 fire control system.  Built by the Hughes Aircraft Company and developed from the E-6 fire control system used by the F-89D, the MG-13 had trouble in controlling the weapons of an aircraft as fast as the F-101B.  Due to the costs involved, the USAF refused to replace the MG-13 with the MA-1 fire control system used by the F-106 Delta Dart.  This led to improvements being made to the MG-13's Central Air Data Computer.[55] Compatible with the Semi-Automatic Ground Environment (SAGE) air defense network, the MG-13 also featured the ability to operate outside the bounds of ground-based radar coverage, a favorable attribute given the range capabilities of the F-101B.

As the F-101B lacked the cannon armament found in the F-101A/C, it relied entirely upon missiles to engage enemy aircraft. The F-101B's missile armament was mounted upon a unique rotating pallet platform located on the aircraft's underside just behind the nose gear and below the rear cockpit.  Such an

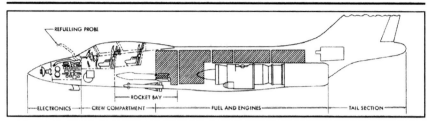

A general diagram illustrating the placement of the F-101B's weapons bay and other major features. (USAF)

arrangement allowed the F-101B to carry three Hughes GAR-1D (AIM-4A) semi-active radar homing (SARH) and three GAR-2A (AIM-4C) infrared homing (IR) Falcon air-to-air missiles on each sortie. Although this represented the most common missile loadout carried by the F-101B during its early career, it was also possible to arm the aircraft with six missiles of either type.[56] Three of the Falcons were carried in a semi-recessed arrangement on the exposed side of the rotary weapon pallet, requiring them to be lowered on launch rails when fired. On the opposite side of the pallet, three additional missiles were mounted on fixed rails as they were carried internally until being fired. The two-sided rotary weapon pallet was able to rotate at an approximate rate of 180-degrees per second.

Late production F-101Bs incorporated a modified pallet arrangement that allowed for the external carriage of two nuclear -armed MB-1 (AIR-2A) Genie rockets and two Falcons internally. The Douglas Aircraft Company began development of the MB-1 during 1954, with the first test firings beginning the following year. The Genie became operational with the USAF in 1957, and was the first air-to-air weapon ever fielded with a nuclear warhead.[57] Possessing no guidance system to home in on a target, the Genie relied upon its 1.5-kiloton warhead's 1,000-foot lethal blast radius to ensure a kill.[58] The F-101B was one of two aircraft belonging to the Century Series that became operational with the Genie during its career, the other being the F-106 Delta

Dart. The capability to carry the MB-1 Genie was retrofitted into many early production F-101Bs beginning in 1961 during Project Kitty Car.

On January 5, 1959, the 60th Interceptor Squadron based at Otis Air Force Base, Massachusetts became the first Air Defense Command unit to become operational with the F-101B. By December of the following year, the F-101B Voodoo was serving in no less than seventeen ADC squadrons.[59] The final F-101B was delivered to the Air Force in March 1961.

Of the 480 F-101 interceptors built, 79 were delivered with dual flight controls for use as operational and conversion trainers. The dual-control aircraft were externally identical to other F-101Bs and retained the same combat weapons systems and capabilities found in the standard B model. These aircraft were first identified as F-101Fs in 1961 as arrangements were being made to transfer 66 of them to the Royal Canadian Air Force.[60] Furthermore, a number of F-101Bs not upgraded to later

A formation of three F-101Bs in flight. Note the long afterburner sections of the interceptor version of the Voodoo. (USAF)

standards were modified by the Air Force with dual flight controls and redesignated as TF-101Bs.[61] In April 1960, several dual-control Voodoos were allocated to the Tactical Air Command to assist in the training of tactical reconnaissance pilots.

Beginning in 1963, under a program known as Project Bold Journey, many F-101B/Fs received an infrared sensor in front of the cockpit following the removal of the retractable air-to-air refueling probe. Between 1963 and 1966, the Interceptor Improvement Program saw the Air Defense Command's F-101B/F fleet receiving upgrades to improve its ability in engaging low-flying targets and in defeating enemy electronic countermeasures. In April 1968, the USAF agreed to the installation of a modification kit to the pitch control system of the F-101B/F's Honeywell MB-5 automatic flight control system. This followed several years of operational difficulties experienced by aircrews with the deficient pitch control system.[62]

In 1969, the first Air National Guard units began receiving the F-101B as the type was withdrawn from active duty USAF squadrons. The first Guard units to receive the F-101B were Maine's 132nd FIS and the state of Washington's 116th FIS when they began receiving Voodoo interceptors in November 1969. The 60th and 62nd Fighter Interceptor Squadrons became the final active duty USAF units to operate the F-101B when they were deactivated on April 30, 1971.[63]

In Air National Guard service, the F-101B found a second career serving primarily in squadrons located in northern states such as Maine, Minnesota, Oregon, New York, and North Dakota, although the type also served in units belonging to the Texas and Nevada ANGs as well. The F-101B served with the Air National Guard for twelve years prior to its retirement in 1981, a length of service virtually identical to its career in active USAF squadrons.

Other than the US Air Force, the only other nation to operate the interceptor version of the Voodoo was the Royal Canadian Air Force (RCAF).[64] The rationale behind the Canadian government's decision to acquire the F-101B for its air defense requirements are outside of the scope of this book, however, a primary reason for this was the cancellation of the Avro CF-105 Arrow interceptor in February 1959, a decision that remains controversial in Canada to this day.

Between July 1961 and through May of the following year, the RCAF received 56 F-101Bs and 10 F-101F dual seat trainers. All of these aircraft were acquired second-hand from the US Air Force, and while in Canadian service, the F-101Bs and the F-101Fs were redesignated as CF-101Bs and CF-101Fs respectively. Following their arrival in Canada, these aircraft were assigned long-range interceptor duties under control of the North American Air Defense Command (NORAD). In 1961, negotiations between the United States and Canada began

This RF-101B (57-0301) served as the prototype for a two-seat reconnaissance version of the Voodoo. This was the only such aircraft converted that had not previously served with Canadian Air Force. (USAF)

concerning the deployment of the AIR-2A Genie rocket on Canadian Voodoo interceptors. These talks continued for two years before an agreement was finally reached and beginning in 1965, the CF-101B's armament included the nuclear-armed AIR-2A. Although deployed operationally to Canadian airbases, the actual control of the Genie's warheads remained the responsibility of US Air Force personnel.

While operating the CF-101B, the 425 Squadron utilized the Voodoo as an aerobatic display aircraft for its flight demonstration team, the Warlocks. Based at CFB Bagotville, near Saguenay, Quebec, the Warlocks performed aerial displays using four CF-101Bs at air shows during the 1970s.

During the 1970-71 timeframe, under Operation Peach Wings, surviving CF-101B/Fs from the original batch acquired during the early 1960s were traded back to the United States for 56 F-101Bs and 10 F-101Fs. The refurbished Voodoos acquired in this transaction had received all of the Bold Journey modifications, including the fitting of IR sensors.

Following their return to the United States, twenty-two of the CF-101Bs, were modified into reconnaissance aircraft by the Martin Marietta Corporation.[65] Designated as RF-101Bs, this variant was operated by the 192nd TRS of the Nevada ANG. The RF-101B was fitted with three KS-87B still cameras and two AXQ-2 television cameras. The service life of the RF-101B was to be short-lived, however, as it was withdrawn from service in 1975.

Meanwhile, CF-101B/Fs continued to perform steadfast service with the Canadian Forces Air Command throughout the 1970s and into the early 1980s. In April 1980, the Canadian government decided upon a successor for the Voodoo when it placed an order with McDonnell Douglas for 138 CF-18A/B Hornets. Furthermore, Air Command's acquisition of the multi-role Hornet was also intended to replace the CF-104 Starfighter and the CF-5 Freedom Fighter.[66] The last Canadian Voodoo squadron stood down in early 1985, although a pair of aircraft modified with ECM gear enabling them to operate as aggressors, and unofficially designated as EF-101Bs, remained active until 1986 when they too were retired, thus bringing to a close the Voodoo's operational career.[67]

Today, some thirty-years following the type's retirement from active duty, a large number of F-101s remain preserved in the United States and Canada as gate guards and museum displays, while in Taiwan a handful serve in similar roles. The Voodoo's design would in some part influence McDonnell's next production fighter, the F-4 Phantom II, one of the most successful fighters of the Cold War era.

# Chapter Three
## Convair F-102 Delta Dagger

Throughout history, wars have served as a catalyst for expediting technological progress. During the Second World War, several advancements in a wide array of technologies took place within a relatively short period of time, most of which would have taken considerably longer to come to fruition had it not been for the expediencies brought upon by the war. An example of this was the extensive research undertaken in Germany concerning jet aircraft and rocket development.

Following the fall of Nazi Germany in 1945, the victorious Allies instituted large-scale operations to seize the volumes of information that the German war industry had created concerning advanced weaponry. Since Germany was many years ahead of its wartime enemies in several key technologies, the acquisition of this data was extremely important to the governments of Britain, Russia, and the United States following the end of the war.

As part of Operation Paperclip, the postwar American program to recruit German scientists, Dr. Alexander Lippisch arrived in the United States. Lippisch, a gifted aeronautical engineer, had begun working on the delta wing concept during the late-1930s.[1] In 1937, the German Air Ministry (RLM) approached Dr. Lippisch, to design an aircraft to test a newly developed rocket motor. Although an initial attempt involving Heinkel had proven unsuccessful, Lippisch later teamed up with

Messerschmitt and developed the Me 163 Komet, surely one of the most unique aircraft to enter service during World War II.[2]

In the United States, prior to the war, the National Advisory Committee for Aeronautics (NACA) had conducted studies of the delta wing concept, and determined that such a wing would possess a very low aspect ratio, thus permitting high speeds.[3] In 1945, after reviewing information concerning Dr. Lippisch's delta wing research, the engineering department at Convair found much promise in the concept for the further development of supersonic aircraft. It was during September of that same year that the US Army Air Forces issued a requirement for a supersonic day interceptor capable of reaching 700 mph in level flight along with a rate of climb enabling it to reach 50,000 feet within 4 minutes after takeoff.[4] At the time, these specifications represented exceptional goals, especially when considering that the first manned supersonic flight had not yet taken place, a feat that would not occur until two years later.

After beating out competing designs from Bell, Northrop, and Republic, the Air Materiel Command named Convair the winner of the interceptor competition on April 12, 1946. In May, Convair received a contract to continue design and development of what was by then termed the XP-92, along with the construction of full -scale engineering mock-up.[5] As wind tunnel testing continued, however, engineers at Convair discovered that the original XP-92 configuration incorporating a conventional fuselage, swept wings, and a V tail arrangement produced disappointing results. This necessitated a complete redesign of the aircraft, resulting the in the adoption of the delta wing to correct these deficiencies. Following the necessary revisions, the new XP-92 design resulted in a strange looking craft that appeared to more as something out of science fiction rather than a practical interceptor aircraft. In November 1946, the USAAF ordered two prototypes of the revised XP-92, along with a full-scale flying model to validate the design's aerodynamic characteristics. To differentiate the experimental aircraft from the XP-92 it was designated as the XP-92A (Convair Model 7-002).[6]

By April 1948, Convair had completed the mock-up of the rocket/ramjet powered XP-92, and was anticipating that the first aircraft would be completed by early 1949. Just a few months later, in August 1948, the USAF cancelled the program. Despite this decision, however, work on the full-size aerodynamic model, which by this time had been redesignated as the XF-92A, continued.

In an effort to reduce the cost and time necessary to develop the XF-92A, its construction incorporated many existing components from other aircraft. On September 18, 1948, the XF-92A Dart flew for the first time, thus becoming the first delta-

The XF-92A (46-0682) was the world's first jet powered delta-wing aircraft to fly. The Dart is shown here in its original bare metal finish. (USAF)

winged jet aircraft to fly. This aircraft was subsequently delivered to the Air Force on May 14, 1949.[7] Severely underpowered by an Allison J33-A-23 engine capable of producing only 5,200 pounds of thrust, the Dart was later fitted with an afterburning equipped Allison J33-A-29 turbojet that could generate up to 8,200 pounds of thrust. However, even with the added power of the new engine, the Dart was unable to exceed Mach 1.0 in level flight.[8] The XF-92A, however, managed to produce invaluable information concerning delta-winged flight until its test program ended following a minor landing mishap in October 1953.

In 1947, the Soviet Union unveiled the Tu-4 Bull bomber to the world during a flyover that took place during Aviation Day festivities in Moscow. This aircraft was a reverse-engineered copy of the Boeing B-29 Superfortress. The manufacture of the Tu-4 had been made possible through the seizure of a small number of damaged American B-29 bombers that landed in Soviet territory during the Second World War while Russia was still neutral with Japan. Although quickly becoming obsolete from a technological standpoint in the era of the jet, the piston powered Tu-4 nonetheless represented a significant danger to US military planners with cities such as Chicago and New York being within its range on one-way missions.[9]

Recognizing the growing capability of the Soviet strategic bomber fleet, the Air Force issued an Advanced Development Objective (ADO) for an advanced interceptor on January 13, 1949.[10] Officially designated Weapon System 201A (WS-201A), this project became popularly referred to as the "1954 Interceptor" program in reference to the year that the USAF intended to place the aircraft into service. The decision to develop an interceptor as a component of a complete weapon system package was based upon the belief that it was becoming impractical to develop sophisticated avionic and weapon systems independently and expecting them to function properly when combined into an airframe.

The Electronic Control System (ECS) for the 1954 Interceptor Program was designated Project MX-1179, for which the Air Force invited 18 electronic contractors to submit proposals from which responses were received from Bendix, General Electric, Hughes Aircraft, North American Aviation, Sperry Gyroscope, and Westinghouse. In the end, however, Hughes Aircraft was awarded a contract in October 1950 to develop its proposed MA-1 fire control system, with production scheduled to begin during 1953.

Meanwhile, on June 18, 1950, the USAF issued a requirement for Project MX-1554, the airframe portion of WS-201A. This resulted in nine proposals being submitted by six aircraft manufacturers. Of these, Republic put forth three submissions, North American two, while Chance-Vought, Convair, Douglas, and Lockheed each submitted a single offer. In July of the following year, the field of competitors was reduced to Convair, Republic, and Lockheed, with the latter's proposal being dropped a short time later.[11]

Benefitting from its experience with its XF-92A Dart, Convair's proposal called for a delta-winged aircraft powered by a single Wright J67 turbojet. To reduce drag, this aircraft was to carry all of its armament of missiles and rockets in internal weapon bays.[12] While Convair's proposal represented a departure from contemporary aircraft design, the offering from its rival was even more daring, and in the end too much so for the time. Republic's Model AP-57 (XF-103) design envisioned a highly advanced turbo-ramjet powered aircraft capable of operating at speeds exceeding Mach 3 at altitudes of up to 80,000 -feet. The US Air Force rightfully deemed this project as being too risky of an endeavor to meet the 1954 in service date envisioned by WS-201A, so it was eliminated from the competition, thus making Convair's entry the de facto winner.[13]

On September 11, 1951, Convair received a letter contract for the MX-1554 airframe, officially designated as the F-102. The same agreement authorized the use of the Westinghouse J40 turbojet, pending the availability of the Wright J67. The Air Force's contract stipulated that the F-102, once fitted with the J67 turbojet, was to reach Mach 1.93 at an altitude of 62,000 feet.[14]

In December 1951, realizing that delays being experienced in developing the aircraft's powerplant and fire control system would prevent either from being ready for service by 1954, the Air Force decided to begin production of an interim interceptor powered by the Westinghouse J40. In 1952, this aircraft was designated as the F-102A. The Air Force intended to acquire an improved model under the F-102B designation once the new engine and fire control systems became available. Later, the F-102B became so dissimilar to the A model that it was redesignated as the F-106 in 1956 and is described separately in

The completed number one YF-102 (52-7994) is shown at Convair's San Diego plant just prior to its shipment to Edwards AFB for flight tests. (USAF)

Chapter 6.

When it was determined that the Westinghouse J-40 lacked the thrust necessary for the F-102A to meet its minimum speed and altitude requirements, it was decided to make a switch to the Pratt & Whitney J57 that was scheduled to enter production in February 1953.[15] Meanwhile, it was also decided that the F-102A would be equipped with the Hughes E-9 fire control system in lieu of the delayed MX-1179 (MA-1). The E-9 was a modified version of Hughes E-4, and following a substantial improvement of its capabilities it was redesignated as the MG-3.[16]

Eager to get its advanced interceptor into service, the USAF decided to utilize the Cook-Craigie Plan for its production. Using this concept, a small batch of preproduction aircraft would be built at a low-rate for a flight-test program, during which production tooling and manufacturing processes would be created in order to shorten lead-time once approval to begin full production was received. This process eliminated a lengthy prototype program, while also allowing any issues discovered during flight-testing to be resolved with necessary modifications integrated into the actual manufacturing process prior to entering series production. The danger in utilizing such a technique was that if major design problems were to crop up during the testing process, a significant re-tooling of the production line would be necessary.

In early 1953, as construction of the first aircraft neared completion, serious troubles with the F-102's design were revealed during ongoing wind tunnel testing. The results of these tests indicated that early performance estimates for the aircraft had been optimistic and did not take into full account the drag characteristics of the design throughout the transonic speed range. Worse yet, as it stood, the F-102 would be unable to achieve Mach 1.0 in level flight, a critical design requirement that simply could not be overlooked. Luckily, there was a solution

The first YF-102 at Edwards AFB. From this angle, the similarity between this aircraft and the XF-92A Dart on page 67 is unmistakable. (USAF)

for the drag problems plaguing the F-102 design.

In 1952, while conducting tests in a transonic wind tunnel at NACA's facility at Langley, Virginia, aerodynamicist Richard T. Whitcomb theorized that transonic drag encountered by an aircraft depended upon its cross-sectional area along the direction of flight.[17] Further testing confirmed that reducing an aircraft's cross-section by indenting its fuselage above the wings resulted in a significant reduction in drag. This concept became known as area rule, the details of which were supplied to engineers from Convair working at Langley.[18] It would not be until mid-1953 that Convair, finally convinced of the shortcomings of its original design, agreed to a redesign of the F-102 incorporating the area rule principle.[19]

Even as Convair struggled with the F-102's drag issues and its subsequent redesign, the first of two YF-102s (Model 8-80) was completed at its San Diego plant during September 1953. This aircraft was transported by truck to Edwards AFB, where it would begin the flight-test phase of the program. Powered by a J57-P-11 turbojet, the YF-102's first flight took place on October 24, 1953 with Convair's chief test pilot, Richard L. Johnson at the controls.[20] As expected, the aircraft was unable to exceed Mach 1.0 in level flight. Additionally, severe buffeting was encountered as the aircraft approached Mach 0.9, while a later attempt to reach Mach 1.0 led to the loss of the first YF-102. This occurred on November 2, 1953, a little more than a week following its first flight, when Johnson was forced to eject when he was unable to get his engine restarted after experiencing a flameout on the YF-102's seventh flight. Johnson suffered serious injuries during the incident, while the YF-102 crashed into the ground just short of the runway.

By the beginning of 1954, the flight test program resumed when the second YF-102 took to the air on January 11, 1954. The first pair of aircraft was followed by eight additional revised YF-102s (Model 8-82). Although these YF-102s received various design changes to increase their performance, such as revised intakes and lengthened forward fuselages, none were given the area rule alterations.[21]

Fully aware that the program was in trouble and subject to cancellation, Convair embarked upon a major redesign for the F-102. On November 15, 1954, after four months of frantic work, the first redesigned aircraft incorporating all of the necessary changes to meet the "1954 Interceptor" requirements was rolled out at San Diego. This aircraft was designated as the YF-102A (Model 8-90), and was followed by three further examples. While, the changes made to the F-102 design saved the program, it necessitated a costly retooling of Convair's production line that involved the scrapping or modification of two-thirds of the 30,000 tools originally created for the YF-102.[22]

In April 1954, wind tunnel tests of a revised F-102A lengthened by 7 feet led to the incorporation of an additional 4 foot extension of the fuselage, which was approved by the Air Force in May of that year.[23] The area rule concept called for the fuselage to be pinched between the joining of the wing's leading edge to the fuselage, continuing aft to conclude near the wing's trailing edge. Since the F-102's design was at such an advanced stage prior to applying this change, there was a limit to how much the aircraft's fuselage could be pinched without an even more drastic redesign. When further wind tunnel testing confirmed that the marginal pinching of the aircraft's waist would not be sufficient to achieve the desired results, Convair engineers solved the problem by adding large aerodynamic fairings to both sides of the aft fuselage.[24]

Along with the area rule changes made to the fuselage, the YF-102A also featured redesigned wings and a new canopy. Dubbed Case X wings by engineers at Convair, the newly redesigned wings were thinner than those fitted to the YF-102. The new wing also featured boundary layer fences to improve airflow over the elevons and a fully cambered leading edge with upturned wingtips. As part of the effort to improve the aircraft's center of gravity, the position of the wings and tail was moved 3 feet aft.[25]

A further revision was the switch to the more powerful Pratt & Whitney J57-P-23 turbojet capable of producing 16,000 pounds of thrust. The added power of this engine helped to offset the growing weight of the aircraft that had witnessed the YF-102A becoming some 3,500 pounds heavier than the original YF-102.

After being completed at San Diego during November 1954, the first YF-102A (53-1787) was transported by truck to Edwards AFB. On 20 December, Richard Johnson took the YF-102A into the air for a short test flight that proved uneventful. The following day, with Johnson once again at the controls, the hard

The differences between the YF-102 and the F-102A are evident in this side-by-side comparison. Note the longer nose, redesigned canopy, and area-ruled fuselage of the F-102A on the right, compared to YF-102 on the left. (NASA)

work put into the redesign of Convair's delta wing aircraft paid off when the YF-102A went supersonic, reaching a top speed of Mach 1.22 and altitude of 53,000 feet.

The first flight of a production F-102A (53-1791) occurred on June 24, 1955, with the Air Force giving its new interceptor the name of Delta Dagger on 29 June of the same year. In April 1956, the 327th Fighter Interceptor Squadron at George AFB, California became first operational unit to be equipped with the F-102A.

Production F-102As were 68 feet 3 inches in length, 21 feet 2 inches in height, and had 38 foot 1 inch wingspans. With a cruising speed of 606 mph, the Dagger was capable of reaching a maximum speed of 825mph. When fully loaded, the F-102A had a gross weight of 31,500 pounds.[26] Early in its career, the F-102 became widely known as the "Deuce," a nickname by which the aircraft has been referred to ever since.

As the flight tests continued, it was found that the aircraft was susceptible to flutter and a lack of directional control at high speeds. This was remedied by the fitting of a larger vertical tail beginning with the 26th production F-102A. The new tail measured 3 feet taller and had a surface area of 95 square feet, an increase of nearly 40-percent compared to the original fin design. The approval to proceed with the taller fin was given just one month prior to the F-102A entering operational service. A subsequent program to retrofit the enlarged tail to 25 aircraft already off the production line was also initiated.[27]

Designed for the singular purpose to engage enemy aircraft, the Delta Dagger was a dedicated interceptor platform. Symbolizing the growing belief in missile technology during the timeframe in which it was developed, the F-102 was the first USAF fighter aircraft designed without a gun. The F-102A's primary armament consisted of six Hughes GAR-1 (AIM-4) Falcon missiles. The Delta Dagger was capable of employing several different versions of the Falcon. During the late 1950s, it was common for the F-102A to carry three GAR-1D (AIM-4A) semi-active radar homing and three GAR-2A (AIM-4C) infrared homing missiles.[28] The Falcons were carried internally within three weapon bays built into the underside of the fuselage, with the missiles being lowered on trapeze assemblies for firing.

In addition to guided missiles, early F-102As were also armed with T-214 2.0-inch unguided rockets that were carried in tubes installed inside the four largest weapon bay doors. These rockets, of which up to 36 could be carried, served as a back-up to the Falcons and were intended for use in a last ditch effort to down an enemy intruder. Although their range was limited, the explosive charge contained in just one of these 2.0-inch rockets was sufficient to either destroy or seriously cripple a bomber-sized aircraft. On July 8, 1955, an YF-102A fired 6 Falcons and 24 rockets in less than 10 seconds. In mid-1956, the USAF decided to replace the T-214 rockets with 24 2.75-inch "Mighty Mouse" rockets.[29] In 1963, the installation of launch kits to fire the AIM-26A/B Super Falcon prompted the removal of the rocket armament.[30]

As related earlier, the F-102A was equipped with the Hughes MG-3 fire control system due to the unavailability of the more advanced MX-1179 (MA-1) system then undergoing development. The MG-3 system was later superseded by the MG-10 that was itself a MG-3 incorporating the AN/ARR-44 data link, the AN/ARC-34 UHF communication set, and the MG-1 automatic flight control system.[31]

The MG-10 fire control system had three primary functions. These were to locate enemy targets, steer an intercept course, and control weapons delivery. To engage a target, an F-102A pilot had three options to choose from in order to carry out his attack. First, the MG-10 could steer a radar-lead collision course to a point at which a missile or rocket attack was carried out automatically or under manual control. The other two targeting modes were optical-lead pursuit and optical-pure pursuit, both

Two F-102As (56-1212 & 56-1138) in flight. (USAF)

Three F-102As of the 327th FIS, George AFB, California thunder into the skies on an interception sortie. (USAF)

of which required the employment of the missiles to be performed manually.[32] The minimum time required by the MG-10 between target acquisition and the firing of weapons was roughly 16 seconds. To increase the chances of achieving a kill, a combination of SARH and IR Falcon missiles were fired in salvoes.

Even after entering service, several modifications were made to the F-102A. One of these was the fitting of intake splitter ramps to improve airflow to the J57 engine and to eliminate a high frequency noise in the cockpit. Responding to complaints from pilots experiencing glare issues emanating from the windscreen, Convair devised a solid black splitter screen that when fitted down the vertical center of the windscreen's frame eliminated the glare.[33] The F-102A's speed brakes, located just above the tailpipe at the base of the vertical tail, also received attention by being increased in size by 40 percent.

In May 1957, a revised wing design for the F-102 was test flown for the first time. The Case XX wing, as the new design was called, differed from the Case X wing used in early F-102s by having an increased amount of camber and larger elevons. Since the camber, or droop, ran along the entire leading edge of the new wing to its very tip, the upturned wingtips common with the Case X wing were eliminated. The Case XX wing raised the aircraft's ceiling by 5,000 feet to 55,000 feet and greatly improved maneuverability.[34]

While engineering the new wing design, the main gear undercarriage was also modified so that it was tilted a few degrees forward. This was done to increase the effectiveness of the elevons in getting the nose airborne, thus lowering takeoff speeds.[35] Since these changes were not incorporated on the assembly line until October of 1957, beginning with approximately the 550th aircraft, over half of the F-102s built did not receive the Case XX wing and landing gear modifications as earlier aircraft were not retrofitted.

Realizing that conventional training aircraft could not emulate the unique characteristics of a delta-wing aircraft, the Air Force issued a requirement for a dual-control trainer version of the F-102A in April 1952. Although, the production of this aircraft, designated as the TF-102A, was authorized on September 16, 1953, the type's procurement was placed on hold due to the problems being experienced by the tactical program. Therefore, it would not be until July 1954 when the Air Force finally placed a firm order with Convair for 20 TF-102As.[36] While it was the intention of the Air Force that this aircraft was to serve primarily as a training platform for prospective F-102A pilots, it was to retain the combat interceptor capability of the single seat model. As such, the aircraft could also fill the role of a radar-training platform for interceptor pilots, a task that was being performed by modified World War II-era B-25 Mitchell bombers.

In September 1954, Convair presented a mockup of the TF-102A's forward fuselage to the Mockup Board at their Fort Worth, Texas plant. While developing the TF-102A, Convair decided to utilize a side-by-side seating arrangement rather than

The TF-102A featured a side-by-side seating arrangement for the instructor and student pilots. The bulky appearance of this model compared to the sharp features of the single-seat F-102A led to the type being nicknamed the "Tub." (USAF)

a conventional tandem arrangement common with other jet trainers. This was done to permit a greater interaction between the student and instructor during training on the aircraft's complex systems. The TF-102A was identical to the standard F-102A aft of the cockpit.[37]

The first flight of a TF-102A (54-1351) took place at Edwards AFB on November 8, 1955. At the controls was Convair's Richard L. Johnson, whom had also taken the first YF-102 aloft on its maiden flight just over two years previously. The bulky forward fuselage section of the TF-102A caused the aircraft to have a somewhat ungainly appearance compared to the pointed features of the single-seat F-102A, resulting in it receiving the unflattering nickname, the "Tub."

At 63 feet 4 inches in length, the TF-102A was 5 feet shorter than the F-102A. As can be expected, regardless of the reduced length, the two-seat version was 828 pounds heavier than the single seat interceptor. Powered by a common Pratt & Whitney J57-P-23A engine, the higher weight of the TF-102A caused it to be somewhat slower than the F-102A, its maximum speed being limited to 606 knots (697 mph).[38] Other performance characteristics, however, such as range, fuel load, and service ceiling were virtually identical between the two models. Although its bulbous cockpit section hindered its top speed, the TF-102A was easily able to become supersonic in a shallow dive. The TF-102A's cockpit arrangement consisted of the instructor seated on right side, while the student pilot occupied the left seat.

The TF-102As built were fitted with the original Case X wings and shorter tails common with early F-102As. Following the development of the taller tail and the Case XX wing, however, these modifications were applied to the TF-102A in a method similar to that used with the F-102A. Sharing a high degree of commonality, the TF-102A was affected by many of the same engineering problems experienced by the single-seat model.

Early test flights of the TF-102A revealed the onset of severe buffeting at Mach 0.8. Subsequent testing revealed that flow separation over the TF-102A's bulbous canopy was the cause of this problem.[39] In an effort to correct this issue engineers at Convair redesigned the canopy. Although this succeeded in reducing the buffeting, it restricted pilot visibility so significantly during landing that it was necessary to return to the original canopy design. The buffeting issue was finally overcome through the installation of several small vortex generators around the frame of the canopy and the fitting of a larger tail. The discovery of the buffeting problem prompted the Air Force to order a production halt that lasted from January until June 1956, when the third TF-102A was successfully flight-tested with the canopy and tail modifications.[40]

In early 1955, 28 additional two-seat trainers were ordered by the Air Force, which later gave Convair a letter contract for another 150 TF-102As in December of that year.[41] Later, however, in light of the numerous delays suffered by the program, along with the arrival of the F-106 Delta Dart, the Air Force decided to reduce their total procurement to just 111 aircraft. The last TF-102As were delivered to the USAF during July 1958, some six months behind schedule.[42]

The TF-102A's weapon fit was identical to that of the F-102A, and it was likewise equipped with the Hughes MG-3 fire control system. When the improved MG-10 system became available for the F-102A, however, it was not retrofitted into the TF-102A fleet.[43] The first operational unit to receive the TF-102A was the 4780th Air Defense Wing based at Perrin AFB, Texas. This unit was responsible for conducting pilot training for the F-102A Delta Dagger. The TF-102A also served as a training aircraft for aircrews assigned to pilot Convair's delta winged bomber, the B-58 Hustler. Besides operating out of Perrin, all active F-102A squadrons typically had two TF-102As assigned for training and conversion purposes.

During 1956, the F-102A began entering service with the Air Defense Command with Convair delivering 97 examples of the new interceptor by the end of the year. As deliveries continued, an expansion of F-102A units took place with 15 squadrons becoming operational with the type by the end of 1957.[44] All of these units operated from bases within the continental United States, the majority of them located in northern states.

In August 1957, the 317th FIS relocated from McChord AFB, Washington to Elmendorf AFB in the Territory of Alaska following its transfer to the Alaskan Air Command (AAC).[45] This redeployment represents the first occasion that an F-102A squadron was based outside of the continental United States. The following month, the 31st FIS also arrived at Elmendorf with their F-102s after transferring from Wurtsmith AFB in Michigan.[46] Located near Anchorage, Elmendorf's location, in conjunction with a number of forward bases, allowed the Delta

A F-102A Delta Dagger belonging to the 317th FIS at Elmendorf AFB, Alaska in January 1958. (USAF)

Dagger to operate over a vast area of territory stretching from northern Canada to the Bering Sea.

By the end of 1958, there were 651 TF/F-102As in service with US Air Force. As the Cold War intensified during the late 1950s and early 1960s, F-102 squadrons belonging to the Air Defense Command stood ready to counter the Soviet bomber threat to North America. In June 1958, the first unit to operate the F-102A, the 327th FIS, redeployed from George AFB to Thule Air Base on the northwest shores of Greenland. Located 695 miles north of the Arctic Circle, Thule was the northernmost base operated by the US Air Force. The stationing of the Delta Dagger at Thule permitted the interception of Soviet long-range aircraft operating over the Arctic Ocean, creating a further buffer zone in the defense of North America.

On July 1, 1962, the 57th FIS based at Keflavik, Iceland was transferred from the Military Air Transport Service (MATS) to the Air Defense Command. Trading in their F-89D Scorpions for the F-102A Delta Dagger, this squadron, known as the Black Knights, was one of the USAF's most active interceptor squadrons during the Cold War. The Black Knights operated the F-102A until it transitioned to the McDonnell Douglas F-4C

Phantom II in 1973, thus becoming the last active duty USAF squadron to operate the Dagger. During that time, however, F-102As from the 57th FIS were scrambled on countless occasions to intercept unidentified aircraft. Many of these turned out to be Soviet long-range reconnaissance and bomber aircraft en route to Cuba or operational missions over the Atlantic. The interception of Soviet aircraft allowed for the gathering of intelligence information from which Western defense experts could formulate an assessment of the current state of Soviet military aviation technology. During the early 1970s, increasing tensions between East and West directly led to an increase in the number of interception missions carried out by the Black Knights. During 1970 alone, the 57th FIS intercepted 347 aircraft, many of which were Tu-20 (Tu-95) Bears.

By 1963, some 450 F-102As had received modifications to employ the AIM-26A/B Super Falcon SARH missile, two of which could be carried. This missile was dimensionally larger

The aerodynamic bulges added to the rear fuselage of the F-102A as part of the area-rule modifications are apparent in this view. (USAF)

than the AIM-4 Falcon missiles that constituted the F-102A's primary armament, thus requiring a reworking of the center weapon bay, including the removal of the FFARs. While the AIM-26B was conventionally armed, the AIM-26A was fitted with a nuclear warhead, and was the only guided nuclear-armed air-to-air missile ever deployed by the United States. In total, three Air Defense Command and three Air National Guard Delta Dagger squadrons received the modifications necessary to employ the nuclear Super Falcon.[47] An earlier attempt to arm the F-102A with the MB-1 (AIR-2) Genie nuclear rocket had been shelved in 1957 despite the successful firing of the weapon from an YF-102 in May 1956.[48] Also during 1963, under Project Big Eight, the Y/F-102A fleet received a infrared search and track system which was mounted inside of a transparent globe just in front of the windscreen.

During 1959, the F-106A Delta Dart and F-101B Voodoo began supplanting the Dagger in the Air Defense Command. Following this, the numbers of TF/F-102As in ADC squadrons quickly diminished. In 1960, the first Daggers arrived in Guard units as the Texas Air National Guard began operating the type. During that same year, the number of active ADC squadrons employing the F-102A had dropped from 27 to just 9 units.[49] The Air Defense Command was redesignated as the Aerospace Defense Command on January 15, 1968. By this time, the Keflavik based 57th FIS was the last ADC unit still operating the Dagger, its previously mentioned transition to the F-4C occurring some 5 years later.

Beginning in January of 1959, the Delta Dagger entered service with the United States Air Forces in Europe (USAFE), beginning a length of service that lasted until April 1970. During this timeframe, six separate squadrons operated TF/F-102As in defense of Europe. As can be expected, the majority of these units were stationed in West Germany. This included the 525th

An F-102A intercepting a Soviet Tu-20 (Tu-95) Bear bomber. During the Cold War such encounters were common. (USAF)

FIS at Bitburg AB, 496th FIS at Hahn AB, and the 526th FIS at Ramstein AB. Rounding out the F-102A squadrons assigned to the USAFE was the 32nd FIS operating from Soesterberg AB in the Netherlands, along with the 431st FIS and the 497th FIS that were based in Spain at Zaragoza AB and Torrejon AB respectively.[50]

Prior to their deployment to Europe, Delta Daggers were processed through the Preparation for Overseas Transfer Program. This process included the installation of TACAN gear, and the upgrading of the MG-10 FCS to the FIG-5 configuration. All told, 150 F-102As and 14 TF-102As received processing for European service, which were later transported overseas by aircraft carrier between January 1959 and December 1960.[51]

During 1963, the 526th FIS at Ramstein was heavily committed in the evaluation of the 412L Air Weapons Control System (AWCS) under a project codenamed Gray Ghost. Besides conducting their normal operations, F-102s from the 526th FIS flew nearly half of the 239 sorties that were necessary to validate the 412L AWCS. While assigned to USAFE squadrons, TF/F-102As and their pilots often deployed to Wheelus AB in Libya for training.[52]

While serving in Europe, a number of F-102As were maintained on a constant state of alert. Beginning in November 1964, this involved two aircraft placed on a 5-minute alert status, with eight more on standby. It was standard practice for the two alert F-102As to be in the air within three to five minutes after receiving the initial alarm. The performance of the Delta Dagger was such that it could reach an altitude of 40,000 feet within four and one half minutes after takeoff.[53]

Delta Daggers originally arrived in Europe with a gray paint scheme similar to that used while the aircraft was serving in the Air Defense Command. Beginning in October 1965, the USAFE's TF/F-102A fleet began receiving camouflage colors in common with the Delta Daggers serving in Southeast Asia. The 526th FIS became the last USAFE unit to operate the F-102A when it performed its final mission in the type on April 1, 1970.[54] Following their departure from Europe, many ex-USAFE Daggers were transferred to Air National Guard units.

Besides the USAFE, the Pacific Air Forces (PACAF) also received the F-102 Delta Dagger. The first of seven PACAF squadrons that would ultimately operate the F-102 was the 16th FIS based at Naha AB, Okinawa, which transitioned to the Dagger in March of 1959.[55] During the early 1960s, the United States began deploying military forces to Southeast Asia as part of an effort to prevent the spread of communism throughout the region. The F-102 Delta Dagger would be involved in such movements.

In April 1961, four F-102As arrived at Don Muang Airbase in Thailand following their deployment from Clark Air Base in the Philippines, as part of Operation Bell Tone.[56] The goal of this movement was to reinforce Thailand's air defenses from encroachment by North Vietnamese aircraft. After detecting aircraft operating along the border separating Vietnam and

Beginning in 1965, Delta Daggers assigned to USAFE units began receiving camouflage paint schemes like those deployed to SEA. Here a TF-102A (56-2331) is shown at RAF Alconbury in May 1968. (USAF)

Cambodia, the PACAF kicked off Operation Waterglass on March 22, 1962 by sending 3 F-102As and 1 TF-102A from the 509th FIS to Tan Son Nhut AB in South Vietnam.

As the US Air Force became more heavily committed to the war in Vietnam, additional air assets were brought into the region. November of 1963 witnessed the beginning of Operation Candy Machine, which called for the regular deployment of TF/F-102As into South Vietnam and Thailand. This involved the deployment of aircraft from the 64th FIS to Tan Son Nhut and Da Nang in South Vietnam, while the 509th FIS commenced operations in Thailand from Don Muang and Udorn RTAB.[57]

Despite its primary role being that of an air defense interceptor, F-102s serving in Southeast Asia performed ground attack duties on rare occasions. In 1965, during Project Stove Pipe, F-102s were employed in attacking ground targets located along the main supply route from North Vietnam into the South, the infamous Ho Chi Minh Trail.[58] During night operations, the

F-102's IR scanner was used to locate ground targets that would be attacked using IR Falcon missiles. If a ground target created a large enough radar return, then SARH Falcons could be launched. During the majority of these operations, Dagger pilots were usually unsure of the effectiveness of their attacks, unless secondary explosions were spotted. The F-102 also served in the unlikely fighter-bomber role to attack ground targets with its unguided FFARs, using an optical sight for aiming. It was during one of these missions, that an F-102A was shot down by ground fire on December 15, 1965. The Delta Dagger was also often used as an escort for packages of attack aircraft. One such occasion led to the only air-to-air loss suffered by the F-102 during its service in Southeast Asia.

On February 3, 1968, a pair of F-102As from the 509th FIS lifted off from Udorn tasked with a fighter escort mission over Laos near the North Vietnamese border. As their aircraft were not equipped with radar homing and warning (RHAW) equipment, the F-102A pilots were unaware that a pair of NVAF MiG-21s was shadowing them until one fired an Atoll heat-seeking missile at them. Although the Atoll failed to detonate when it struck the F-102A flown by Lt. Wallace Wiggins, the damage it inflicted led to the aircraft breaking up and killing the pilot. Meanwhile, the second F-102A, piloted by Captain Al Lomax, fired three AIM-4 Falcons at the fleeing MiG-21s, none of which struck their intended targets.[59]

Deployments to PACAF units from the United States involved long distances over the vast Pacific Ocean, a severe handicap to an aircraft unable to be refueled in flight. To rectify this, 87 Delta Daggers were fitted with temporary in-flight refueling probes fitted to the upper right-hand side of the fuselage, extending forward to end alongside the cockpit. This modification enabled the F-102 to be refueled during the long transits over the Pacific, thus shortening deployment lead times. However, this installation degraded the Dagger's performance to such a degree that it was removed after the aircraft had completed its flight across the Pacific.[60]

Initially, F-102s operating in the Far East were painted in a standard gray paint scheme this later being replaced by the tri-tone camouflage pattern that became standard for the type in Southeast Asia. As the air war in Vietnam expanded, and the dangers intensified, the F-102 received modifications to carry an ECM pod, or an AN/ALE-2 chaff dispenser in place of its standard drop tanks. One shortcoming, however, was never rectified, this being the lack of installed RHAW equipment.[61]

In September 1968, Candy Machine deployments of the F-102 to South Vietnam came to a close, which was followed by the end of similar deployments to Thailand in November of the following year. The USAF lost 14 F-102As and 1 TF-102A during operations in Southeast Asia. Eight of these losses, 7 F-102As and 1 TF-102A, were caused by operational accidents. However, 7 F-102As were lost to enemy action during the type's Vietnam War deployment history, this consisting of 2 to ground fire, 4 to sapper attack, and the single air-to-air loss.[62]

Beginning in 1970, the F-4 Phantom II began rapidly replacing the F-102 in PACAF squadrons. The last PACAF squadron to operate the type was the 82nd FIS based at Naha AB, which was inactivated on May 31, 1971. Following their retirement, thirty-five of the Daggers formerly operated by the 82nd FIS were scrapped in-place.

Beginning in July 1960, the F-102 started entering service with Air National Guard units when the 182nd FIS of the Texas ANG transitioned from the F-86L Sabre to the Dagger. Over the next 16 years, no less than 23 Air National Guard squadrons operated both single and dual seat Daggers. All but one of these units was controlled by the Air Defense Command, and its successor the Aerospace Defense Command, the sole exception being the 199th

After being replaced in frontline squadrons by more modern types, many F-102s were transferred to the Air National Guard. Shown here is a F-102A belonging to the 178th FIS of the North Dakota ANG. (DI)

FIS of the Hawaii Air National Guard. Based at Hickam AFB just west of Honolulu, this squadron was assigned to the PACAF. The 199th FIS also became the last Guard operator of the F-102 when it conducted its final sortie with the type in October 1976, just prior to completing its transition to the F-4C. During its time in service with the Air National Guard, forty-four Delta Daggers were lost in accidents.

During its operational career, the F-102 was used to support a wide array of Air Force test programs. While assigned to such duties it was common for these aircraft to receive a temporary JF-102A designation. Besides the USAF, the Dagger was utilized by NACA and its successor, NASA, over a twenty-year period commencing in 1954 and ending in 1974. During this time, nine F-102s were operated by this organization in support of various experimental programs. Among the projects involving the F-102 were the X-20 Dyna-Soar reusable spacecraft program, and the Astronaut Proficiency Flying Program. A single F-102 was acquired by the Federal Aviation Administration (FAA) in 1970 to be used in tests concerning America's SST program. During 1959, General Electric equipped an F-102 (54-1398) to perform as a flying platform for the tests of their J85 turbojet engine that would eventually power the T-38 Talon and a variety of light attack aircraft.

By 1973, the retirement of the F-102 out of USAF and ANG squadrons had created a surplus of some 400 aircraft in storage. Identifying a need for a high-speed target that was capable of emulating enemy aircraft such as the MiG-21, the US Air Force awarded the Sperry-Rand Corporation a contract to convert six of these aircraft into drones at a cost of 5.5 million under Project Pave Deuce. Two of the Daggers were to be converted into QF-102As, which retained flight controls for contractor-operated flights, while the remaining four became PQM-102As that were not rated for manned flight.[63] A further version, the PQM-102B, was a low-cost version of the F-102 drone that featured a cost savings of $100,000 per unit. The first flight of a QF-102A took place on January 10, 1974, followed by the first unmanned PQM-102A flight in August of the same year.[64] When production ended in 1981, some 215 F-102s received drone conversions consisting of 5 QF-102As, 65 PQM-102As, and 145 PQM-102Bs.

The drone conversion process involved the removal of all unnecessary avionics and weapon systems. Following this, a Sperry-Rand Flight Control Stabilization System was installed, as well as a smoke system for ground tracking and a self-destruct device consisting of a MK-48 warhead. Besides the USAF, the US Army utilized 14 PQM-102s during the 1970s while testing the man-portable Stinger missile, as well as the SAM-D, later renamed the Patriot, surface-to-air missile system.

Operations of PQM-102 drones were divided between

Holloman AFB, New Mexico, and Tyndall AFB, Florida. On numerous occasions, PQM-102s returned safely to base after suffering damage, with many of these drones surviving several missions before meeting their final destruction. The QF-102 continued performing missions at Tyndall until July 14, 1983. Pave Deuce operations at Holloman AFB continued for nearly another three years prior to the last mission being flown on June 30, 1986.

The F-102 Delta Dagger also served in the air forces of Greece and Turkey, after supplied second-hand from the United States as part of a Military Assistance Program (MAP) to assist those two nations in meeting their NATO obligations. Except for two TF-102As, all of these aircraft had previously served with the Air National Guard.

The Turkish Air Force (Türk Hava Kuvvetleri) eventually acquired 35 F-102As and 6 TF-102As, after beginning operations with the type in June 1968. The F-102 Delta Dagger represented just one of three Century Series fighters operated by Turkey, the others being the F-100 Super Sabre and the F-104 Starfighter. A year later, in June 1969, Greece's air force, the Royal Hellenic Air Force, received their first Daggers. Greece acquired a slightly smaller fleet of F-102s than Turkey, consisting of 20 F-102As and 4 two-seat TF-102As.

Turkey and Greece are traditional enemies, particularly concerning the Mediterranean island of Cyprus. In July 1974, it was reported that two Hellenic F-5As had shot down a pair of Turkish F-102As during Turkey's invasion of Cyprus. This report was disputed by Turkish claims that their F-102As had actually downed two Greek F-5As instead.[65]

Following its actions against Cyprus, the United States Congress emplaced a military arms embargo against Turkey, which severely hampered that nation's ability to maintain its F-102 force. The Türk Hava Kuvvetleri retired the last of its Delta

Daggers in June 1979. Meanwhile, the Hellenic Air Force had replaced its F-102s the previous year with the Dassault Mirage F1CG.

The F-102 Delta Dagger has one of the most troubled design histories of any of the Century Series fighters. The discovery of serious drag issues with the original design nearly spelt disaster for the program. However, an extensive reworking of the innovative design enabled the Delta Dagger to enter service as a capable air-defense interceptor while also forming the basis for the F-106 Delta Dart, an aircraft often referred to as the "Ultimate Interceptor."

# Chapter Four
## Lockheed F-104 Starfighter

During the Korean War, US Air Force fighter pilots found themselves confronted by Russian built MiG-15s that outclassed the performance of their own F-80 Shooting Stars and F-84 Thunderjets. Only the premier US fighter of the conflict, the North American F-86 Sabre, proved to be a match for the nimble MiG-15. In several ways, the MiG-15 was superior to the F-86, but in the end, the superior training provided to US pilots enabled them to attain a superior kill ratio against their communist adversaries. Following the war, it was believed that US airmen had held a 14:1 margin over their opponents. After further examination, however, this ratio was lowered to 10:1, with later studies suggesting that a 7:1 kill to loss ratio is more accurate.[1]

Among the advantages held by the Soviet fighter were its superior climb rate, heavier armament, and higher ceiling. Air Force fighter pilots came to regard the MiG-15 as being superior to early models of the Sabre at altitudes in excess of 30,000 feet.[2] The F-86 did, however, hold some advantages over its communist adversary, including a better diving capability, excellent low speed stability, and a radar gunsight.

Developed prior to the missile age, both the F-86 and MiG-15 were fitted with guns as their primary armament. In the case of the Sabre, this consisted of six .50-calibre Colt-Browning M-3 machine guns with 267 rounds of ammunition carried for each gun.[3] With the exception of the radar assisted gunsight, the F-86's armament was similar to that fitted to P-51 Mustang which was produced by North American during the Second World War. Meanwhile, the MiG-15 was equipped with a harder-hitting armament consisting of one 37mm and two 23mm cannons. Both of these weapon arrangements had advantages over the other, this primarily being the Sabre's machine guns producing a higher rate of fire, while the MiG-15's cannons ability to deliver a heavier punch was hampered by a slower rate of fire and inferior fire-control systems compared to those available to US pilots.

During the Korean War, Lockheed's Clarence "Kelly" Johnson visited Korea and found that US airmen were looking for a new type of fighter that emphasized outright altitude and speed performance above all else. The top scoring USAAF ace of World War II in the European Theatre, Colonel Francis "Gabby" Gabreski, summed up the frustration felt by US fighter pilots when he commented, "We're burdened by complicated and heavy devices in big, heavy airplanes. I'd rather sight with a piece of chewing gum stuck on the windscreen."[4]

Upon his return to Lockheed's Skunk Works at Burbank, California, Kelly Johnson and his team began working on a series of engineering studies that ultimately led to a design designated L-246 (Model 83). Unlike other US fighters of the era that were becoming increasingly heavier and sophisticated, Lockheed's L-246 design embraced a philosophy envisioning a lightweight aircraft possessing a superior speed and altitude performance that was unburdened with equipment unnecessary for it to fulfill its primary role as a supersonic day fighter.

In November 1952, Lockheed made an unsolicited proposal to the US Air Force when it submitted its L-246 design for consideration as a new air superiority fighter. The Air Force felt that such an aircraft would be necessary to replace its F-100

Super Sabre during the 1956 timeframe and issued a General Operational Requirement (GOR) on December 12, 1952 calling for the development of a lightweight air superiority fighter.[5] Besides Lockheed's L-246, the Air Force received proposals from North American, Northrop, and Republic.[6] In the end, however, the Air Force chose Lockheed's L-246 as the most promising of the four submissions in January 1953. This decision was also based in part by the Air Force's desire to prevent North American or Republic from gaining a monopoly on new fighter aircraft development.

Despite selecting Lockheed's design, the USAF proceeded cautiously with the program. On March 11, 1953, under the auspices of Weapon Systems 303A (WS-303A), the US Air Force issued a letter contract calling for the manufacture of two prototypes of Lockheed's L-246 design designated as XF-104s and one year of flight testing. The initial mockup inspection took place on April 30, 1953, which prompted the replacement of the two original 30mm guns with a single 20mm T-171 (M61 Vulcan) cannon then under development.[7]

Lockheed's new fighter, which was to be named Starfighter, incorporated several unique features that allowed it to achieve the high speed and altitude performance characteristics around which it had been designed. Perhaps the most notable of these was the design of the aircraft's low aspect ratio wings that were unique in an era dominated by swept and delta winged aircraft. Unlike conventional wings, those developed for the XF-104 were short and extremely thin, so thin in fact, that they contained virtually no internal volume.

Results from a testing program involving the Douglas X-3 Stiletto research aircraft had a major influence on the design of the XF-104's wings. The contract to build the X-3 had been awarded to the Douglas Aircraft Company in 1947 through the joint sponsorship of the USAF, the US Navy, and NACA.[8] When the Stiletto took to the air for the first time on October 20, 1952, it had an appearance more in common with a rocket ship than an aircraft due to its long pointed nose and streamlined features. Despite its futuristic looks, however, the aircraft was woefully underpowered and was only capable of exceeding Mach 1.0 in a dive. Although it was unable to perform as anticipated, the X-3 produced important data concerning the performance of thin trapezoidal double-wedge profile wings, and the integrated use of titanium in airframe design. In an effort to minimize its losses associated with the program, the Air Force instructed Douglas to share the information gathered from the project with Lockheed.[9]

The wing design chosen for the F-104 was well suited for supersonic flight performance, however, such wings possessed two significant disadvantages. First, the extreme thinness of the wings prevented their use for fuel carriage, thus requiring all of the aircraft's fuel tanks to take up valuable space within the fuselage. Although the fitting of external drop tanks on the

The Douglas X-3 Stiletto research aircraft. The data produced by this aircraft assisted in the design of the F-104's wings. (NASA)

wingtips would offset this deficiency to some degree, it reduced the offensive capability of the aircraft by preventing the mounting of Sidewinder missiles on those same stations. Secondly, besides being razor-thin, the wings also possessed a small surface area equal to 196.1 square feet. This gave the aircraft a very high wing loading factor that limited its maneuverability. A further consequence of the Starfighter's wing design was that its leading edge was so sharp that the placement of protective covers was required to prevent injuries to members of the ground crew while the aircraft was on the ground during servicing.

With a maximum depth of only 4.2 inches, the wings presented significant technical difficulties for engineers at Lockheed while designing actuator units for the aircraft's control surfaces. In one such example, the actuator unit created to drive the outboard ailerons consisted of a row of ten small hydraulic rams placed inside of a solid block of aluminum that was restricted to a 1.1-inch thickness. These units were developed by Lockheed in cooperation with the Bertea Corporation, and were known as piccolo actuators.[10]

To improve the effectiveness of its stubby wings during approach and landing, the Starfighter was the first production aircraft to be equipped with a Boundary Layer Control System (BLCS). Such a system functions by allowing high-pressure air to be bled from the engine, which is then blown through slits ahead of the upper surfaces of the flaps.[11] This process generates additional lift at low speeds, thereby reducing the landing speed of an aircraft with a high wing loading factor. To generate additional lift during takeoff and landing, the wings were also fitted with full-span leading edge flaps that were equipped with electrical actuators that allowed them to droop downwards.

After studying several different tail configurations, it was decided to mount the all-flying tailplane on the very top of the vertical fin. This was done in an effort to improve lateral stability by placing it outside of the turbulence created by the wings and the fuselage. The tailplane moved as one piece and was not fitted with any elevators. The Starfighter's high tail made its vertical fin very effective, so much so that it acted much like a wing during rolling turns. To offset this tendency, engineers at Lockheed gave the wings a negative dihedral.[12]

For Kelly Johnson and his design team, the use of a T-tail configuration created some concern towards pilot safety during a high-speed ejection. Believing that contemporary ejection seat systems did not possess the capability of clearing the F-104's tail assembly during such an ejection led to the decision to fit the Starfighter with a downward firing ejection seat. The initial version of this ejection system fitted to the XF-104 prototypes, and early Starfighters, was the Stanley B seat.

A downward firing ejection system had a number of disadvantages, the most obvious being that it was ineffectual at low altitudes. Since a large percentage of early jet fighter aircraft accidents had occurred at low altitude or during takeoff and landing, such an ejection seat proved to be very unpopular with Air Force pilots. The Stanley B seat was superseded by the C and C-1 seats, both of which were improved versions of the downward firing seat. The deficiencies of this type of escape method prompted the development of the Lockheed C-2 upward firing ejection seat. While this seat type greatly improved the chances of a pilot's survival, it still had its limitations, in particular its 104 mph minimum speed requirement.

To power the XF-104, Lockheed chose a license built version of the British Armstrong Siddeley Sapphire turbojet, the Wright YJ65-W-6. Equipped with an afterburner, this turbojet had a 15,000 pound maximum thrust rating. This powerplant, however, would not be initially available to power the XF-104s, thus forcing the installation of a non-afterburning version of the

J65 that was capable of only producing 10,200 pounds of thrust.[13]

After its completion at Burbank, the first XF-104 (53-7786) was transported by road to Edwards AFB, where it began its taxi tests during February 1954. On 28 February, Lockheed's chief test pilot Tony LeVier made a short hop into the air over a distance of about 300 feet before setting the aircraft back down on the dry lakebed. On March 4, 1954, LeVier took the XF-104 Starfighter into the skies above Edwards on its first official flight.[14]

In July 1954, the afterburning Wright J65-W-7 turbojet became available, allowing the replacement of the original non-afterburning J65 that had powered the number one XF-104. While this permitted the aircraft to achieve a level speed of Mach 1.49, it still prevented the Mach 2.0 performance that Lockheed was striving to obtain with the design. The fastest flight of an XF-104 occurred on March 25, 1955 when the number two aircraft, piloted by Lockheed test pilot J. Ray Goudey, reached a speed of Mach 1.79. Neither of the XF-104s was fitted with the Boundary Layer Control System (BLCS) that was standard with production Starfighters.

On October 5, 1954, the second XF-104 (53-7787) embarked upon its maiden flight. This aircraft was fitted with the

The first XF-104 (53-7786) at Edwards AFB. Note the type's T-tail configuration, short fuselage, and lack of inlet shock cones. (USAF)

101

The first XF-104 in flight. This aircraft was designed as a lightweight jet fighter possessing outstanding performance capabilities. (USAF)

afterburning J65 right from the beginning and since it was to be utilized as an armament test bed it also had a M61 Vulcan cannon and a AN/ASG-14T-1 fire control system installed. The number two aircraft would suffer a pair of in-flight incidents while performing gun trials, one of which would lead to its destruction.

On December 17, 1954, as Tony LeVier was firing the 20mm cannon, the number two XF-104 shuddered as a small explosion occurred within its fuselage. At about the same moment, the J65 engine began experiencing compressor stalls forcing LeVier to shut it down. Fortunately, he was able to guide the XF-104 down to a dangerous deadstick landing on Rogers Dry Lake. A subsequent investigation revealed that a 20mm round had exploded inside of the breech, causing the gun's firing bolt to be blown backwards into the forward fuel cell. This resulted in the expelling of large amounts of jet fuel directly into the face of the engine, thus causing the onset of the compressor stalls.

A second incident befell this aircraft during armament trials on April 14, 1955 while piloted by Herman "Fish" Salmon. As Salmon was firing the M61 Vulcan at an altitude of 50,000 feet, his XF-104 suddenly experienced a series of severe vibrations following a malfunction in the gun. The shaking of the aircraft was intense enough to cause the bottom panel of the downward firing ejection seat to come loose, thereby leading to a sudden loss of pressure in the cockpit. When Salmon's pressure suit inflated to compensate for the change in air pressure, it covered his face and by doing so cost him the ability to see. Aware of the loss of power experienced by LeVier during the previous gun malfunction, Salmon reasoned that he was facing a similar circumstance and since he was unable to see clearly enough to attempt a powerless landing, made the decision to eject. Although Salmon was able to safely parachute to the ground, the incident resulted in the destruction of the number two XF-104. A later investigation determined that the aircraft may have been safely recovered had Salmon waited until reaching a lower altitude which would have allowed his pressure suit to deflate.[15]

Following the loss of the second XF-104, the sole remaining prototype continued conducting flight test work as the Starfighter program matured. Meanwhile, modifications were made to a F-94C Starfire to allow the testing of the Starfighter's armament and fire control systems to continue.[16] The first XF-104 was accepted by the Air Force in November 1955, and continued flying until July 11, 1957 when it crashed following the loss of its tail section resulting from an uncontrollable tail flutter. Piloting the XF-104 on its final flight that day was Lockheed test pilot Bill Park whom survived the accident when he ejected safely before the aircraft plunged to the ground.

In September 1954, the first XF-104 completed Phase I testing. On March 30, 1955, the Air Force ordered 17 service test examples of the Starfighter designated as YF-104As.[17] These aircraft differed from the XF-104s in being designed to accommodate the new General Electric J79 turbojet. Measuring 54 feet 8 inches in length, YF-104As were 5 feet 6 inches longer than the XF-104s. Other design changes incorporated into the YF-104A included a forward retracting nose wheel and a fairing running along the aircraft's spine. Additionally, the intakes were increased in size and fitted with half-cones to position the oblique shock wave that formed at supersonic speeds.[18]

Apprehensive that the General Electric J79 turbojet would be available in time, the Air Force considered the option of using the J65 for early F-104s. However, ongoing problems with that engine soon eliminated this possibility. In December 1955, flight-testing of the XJ79-GE-3 using a borrowed US Navy XF-4D reassured the Air Force that it would be available in time to power the YF-104A.[19]

On December 23, 1955, the first YF-104A (55-2955) was rolled out at Burbank, and after being transported to Edwards AFB, it flew for the first time on February 17, 1956. The maiden flight of the YF-104A ended prematurely when test pilot Herman Salmon began experiencing problems with its J79 engine that prompted him to bring the aircraft in for a landing.[20] This aircraft was joined by a second YF-104 which entered the flight test program during June of that year.

Early YF-104As were fitted with the General Electric J79-GE-3 axial-flow turbojet that had a dry thrust rating of 9,300 pounds and 14,800 pounds with afterburning. Later YF-104As were equipped with the J79-GE-3A, which featured improved reliability.[21] The increased thrust of the J79 engine allowed the fleet of YF-104A service test aircraft to achieve the design's true performance capabilities. On April 27, 1956, this was aptly demonstrated when a YF-104A reached a speed of Mach 2.13, thus becoming the first Air Force jet fighter possessing a doublesonic capability.

Of the seventeen YF-104As built, at least two were lost in accidents during the flight test program. In one instance, an YF-104A was lost when its external fuel tanks collided with its tail after being jettisoned from the wingtip stations.[22] Another YF-104A was lost during testing to a aerodynamic phenomenon known as a deep stall.[23] In simple terms, a deep stall occurs when turbulent air generated by the wings during a loss of lift at high angles of attack envelops the horizontal stabilizer therefore rendering the elevators ineffectual. Aircraft incorporating a T-tail configuration, such as the F-104, are highly vulnerable to entering into this type of stall.

A variety of unexpected difficulties led to the expansion of the testing program in 1956 to include the first 35 F-104As built. One of the most significant issues encountered during testing concerned the reliability of the J79 engine, which included the turbojet's vulnerability to flameouts, ignition failures, and oil depletions. Such engine deficiencies were factors in a number of

A front view of an F-104 illustrates the negative dihedral of the Starfighter's extremely thin wings. The edges of these wings were so sharp that protective covers were necessary to prevent injuries to ground personnel. (USAF)

in-flight emergencies and crashes during both testing and the type's initial entry into operational service.[24]

As the F-104A's in-service date continued to slip during 1956, the Tactical Air Command (TAC) began losing interest in the Starfighter. This was further exacerbated by the type's relatively small payload capability and limited range, which severely restricted its usefulness as a tactical fighter. However, at the same time, the Air Defense Command (ADC) was looking for a fighter to fill the gap between its F-102 Delta Dagger and F-106 Delta Dart interceptors. Lacking an all-weather capability, compounded by its inability to integrate with the Semi-Automatic Ground Environment (SAGE) air defense network made the F-104A somewhat ill suited to serve in the interceptor role. The Starfighter's speed and rate of climb capabilities, however, made it attractive to the ADC as a point defense fighter. In April 1956, this led to a shift in the acquisition of the F-104 away from the TAC and towards the ADC.[25] Coincidentally, the Air Force decided to equip the Starfighter with the GAR-8 (AIM-9) Sidewinder around this same timeframe. Furthermore, the Tactical Air Command also made the decision to cancel a proposed reconnaissance version of the type, the RF-104A.[26]

The F-104A entered operational service on January 26, 1958 when the Air Defense Command's 83rd FIS based at Hamilton AFB, near San Francisco became the first unit to receive the type.[27] Due to technical difficulties encountered during its development, the arrival of the Starfighter into operational squadrons had taken two years longer than originally planned.

Production of the F-104A concluded in December 1958 with the delivery of the last eight aircraft to the Air Force. Including the YF-104As, 170 examples of the A model were produced, far less than the 610 the USAF had originally planned to acquire in 1957. While funding shortages accounted for most of this reduction, an underlying factor was that the leadership of the

Two F-104As (56-0769 & 56-0781) in flight. Both aircraft are carrying AIM-9 Sidewinder air-to-air missiles. (USAF)

USAF was unconvinced of the need for a lightweight fighter. To the contrary, the Air Force was moving towards larger and increasingly more sophisticated aircraft such as the F-105 and the F-106.

Shortly after entering service, the "Zipper" or "Zip 104" as it became known by its USAF pilots, was involved in a number of accidents caused by its J79-GE-3A engine. This prompted the Air Force to ground all of its F-104As in April 1958, just three months after the type had first entered service. To address shortcomings with its J79 engine, General Electric developed a more reliable version designated as the J79-GE-3B, which was retrofitted into early F-104As beginning in April 1958.[28] Despite being fitted with a more dependable engine, the Starfighter continued to compile a poor safety record when compared to other aircraft belonging to the Century Series.[29] Despite its dubious reputation, however, the F-104A was able to accomplish a number of notable achievements during its early career.

On May 7, 1958, Major Howard C. Johnson established a new world altitude record when he took his YF-104A to an altitude of 91,243 feet. The setting of a new world speed record occurred nine days later when another YF-104A flown by Captain Walter W. Irwin reached a speed of 1,404.09 mph on May 16, 1958. Following these record setting flights, the Lockheed Starfighter became the first aircraft to hold both the world's altitude and speed records simultaneously.

The F-104A's armament consisted of what were then two recently developed air-to-air weapons, these being the 20mm M61 Vulcan cannon and the AIM-9 Sidewinder missile. These weapon systems have become two of the most prolific postwar aerial weapons produced by the United States with advanced versions of both still in production to this day.

The M61 originated from a US Army contract placed with General Electric in 1946 to develop a Gatling-type gun that possessed a remarkable rate of fire while also being extremely reliable. After a great deal of experimentation, a design designated as the T171 was tested in 1952 using 20 x 102mm cartridges, which had been determined as having the proper combination of muzzle velocity and hitting power. Later

A ground view of a F-104A (56-0758) illustrates the type's undercarriage arrangement. (USAF)

redesignated as the M61 Vulcan, the F-104 Starfighter was the first production aircraft to be fitted with this weapon. The single M61 cannon was installed just behind the pilot in the lower left side of the fuselage and fired through a gun port located directly below the cockpit. The electrically operated gun had an average rate fire of 4,000 rounds per minute and carried 725 rounds of 20mm ammunition.[30]

The six-barreled M61 used linked ammunition that led to some concerns regarding its use in the F-104. The most obvious danger stemming from the use of such an ammunition feed system was the potential for the aircraft to sustain foreign object damage from discarded links. To avoid this possibility, an improved version of the gun that featured link less ammunition was later developed and designated as the M61A1. Initially, the M61 had a troubled history in the F-104 that included heavy vibrations being experienced during firing and an occasional premature detonation of its 20mm ammunition. Considering the M61 too unreliable for operational use in early F-104s, the Air Force prohibited the fitting of weapon into the aircraft during November 1957, pending the resolution of its deficiencies. The F-104A operated without a gun until 1964 when the improved M61A1 became available. Besides the F-104, only one other Century Series fighter, the Republic F-105 Thunderchief, was designed to be equipped with the Vulcan cannon. Subsequent lessons garnered from the air war over Vietnam, however, prompted the installation of a podded version of the M61 into some F-106 Delta Darts during the early 1970s.

The F-104A was capable of carrying a pair of GAR-8 (AIM-9B) Sidewinder IR missiles on its wingtip stations in place of the standard 165-gallon drop tanks. The Sidewinder was successfully fired for the first time on September 11, 1953. The GAR-8 was the initial production version of the Sidewinder, which after 1963 was redesignated as the AIM-9B. Armed with a

The F-104B was a two-seat training version of the F-104A and flew for the first time on January 16, 1957. (USAF)

10 pound high-explosive warhead, both the USAF and the US Navy purchased this missile for use with their fighter aircraft. The AIM-9B measured 9 feet 3 ½ inches in length and had a launch weight of 159 pounds.[31]

When fired, an AIM-9B accelerated to a speed of Mach 2.5 in just 2.2 seconds. With an effective range of only 2 miles, the Sidewinder was steered towards its target by a set of four control fins located just behind the seeker head. Since the AIM-9B's seeking ability was limited to homing onto an aircraft's engine exhaust, the Starfighter's pilot was required to maneuver into a position just behind an adversary prior to firing. Development of the AIM-9B took place at China Lake, California by the Naval Ordnance Test Station (NOTS). Domestic production of the AIM -9B was first performed by Philco and later General Electric. During its production run, these two firms delivered an estimated 80,900 examples of this Sidewinder model, which when combined with 15,000 additional missiles produced in Europe makes the AIM-9B one of the most widely used air-to-air missiles used by the West during the Cold War.[32]

During a testing program to equip the Starfighter with the MB -1 (AIR-2A) Genie rocket, at least one F-104A (56-0749) received modifications allowing it to carry the nine-foot long nuclear-armed weapon. This involved the installation of a trapeze mounting on the aircraft's underbelly just behind the nose gear doors. In preparation for firing, the trapeze extended to avoid fouling the J79 engine with the Genie's rocket exhaust. Although at least one live firing of an inert MB-1 took place, the F-104A never reached an operational status with the weapon.

In December 1955, the Air Force decided to acquire a two-seat training version of the F-104A designated as the F-104B. After issuing an initial order for 6 F-104Bs in April 1956, the Air Force ordered an additional 106 examples the following year.[33] The F-104B flew for the first time on January 16, 1957, with the Air Force accepting delivery of this aircraft later that month. While there was a high degree of commonality between the F-104A and the two-seat B model, the addition of a second cockpit forced the deletion of the M61 cannon and a reduction in the internal fuel load, the latter corresponding to a significant decrease in range compared to the A model. Although the F-104B lacked an internal gun, its ability to carry two AIM-9B Sidewinders on its wingtips remained identical to that of F-104A. Moreover, the AN/ASG-14T-1 fire control system from the single seat model was also retained. Both of the F-104B's cockpits were equipped with a full set of flight controls.

During 1958, the 83rd FIS at Hamilton AFB became the first squadron to operate the F-104B. For pilot proficiency and transitional training purposes, a small number of F-104Bs were assigned to each of the ADC's four F-104A squadrons. Despite having some 112 F-104Bs on order during 1957, the USAF later slashed its procurement to just 26 examples with the last four aircraft being delivered in November 1958. The first batch of six F-104Bs retained the same vertical stabilizer used in standard F-

A Lockheed F-104A (56-0791) is shown on September 15, 1958, while deployed to Taiwan during the Quemoy Crisis. (USAF)

104As. This was changed, however, when an instability issue discovered during testing revealed the need for a tail with a larger surface area. Therefore, the last twenty F-104Bs built incorporated an enlarged tail to improve the type's stability.

With the F-104A/B's inherit limitations in fulfilling the interceptor role, combined with budgetary constraints, it is not surprising that the Starfighter's initial length of service with the ADC was relatively brief. Following the arrival of F-101B and F-106 Delta Dart interceptors during 1959, the Air Defense Command phased the F-104A out of squadron service by the end of the following year, a length of service equating to just less than three years.

In 1958, the ADC deployed a small number of its F-104As to Taiwan to bolster that nation's air defenses during the Quemoy Crisis.[34] This move was a component of an effort made by the United States to demonstrate its support for Republic of China (Taiwan) against the People's Republic of China (PRC). The crisis began on August 23, 1958 when the PRC began a massive artillery barrage against a group of islands collectively known as Quemoy. This resulted in a significant US military build up on Taiwan, which included the dispatching of 12 F-104As from the 83rd FIS at Hamilton AFB. Lacking an aerial refueling capability, the F-104As were broken down and flown to Taiwan aboard USAF Douglas C-124 Globemaster transports. The first of these transports arrived in Taiwan on September 10, 1958.

Following the arrival of the first F-104 in Taiwan, a herculean effort took place to reassemble the fighters, the first of which was airborne within 24 hours of its crated arrival. As the deployment of the Starfighters continued, personnel from 337th FIS arrived to assume the duties of the 83rd FIS, while continuing to operate the same aircraft originally deployed.[35] Air Defense Command F-104As continued operating from Taiwan throughout the duration of the crisis, which ended with a cease-fire agreement on October 6, 1958 without the Starfighter being involved in any hostile aerial engagements before returning to the United States.

Following their removal from ADC squadrons, F-104A/Bs were transferred to three separate units of the Air National Guard. These were the 151st FIS of the Tennessee ANG, the 157th FIS of the South Carolina ANG, and the 197th FIS of the Arizona ANG. In October 1961, all three of these squadrons deployed to Europe following being called to active duty in response to the Berlin Wall Crisis. After tensions eased, the F-104s returned to the United States during the summer of 1962. In a strange turn of events, however, the Starfighter returned to the Air Defense Command to serve with the 319th and the 331st FIS Fighter Interceptor Squadrons based at Homestead AFB and Webb AFB respectively.[36]

The primary reason behind the F-104A/B's return to the Air Defense Command was the threat posed by the arrival of Soviet built jet fighter aircraft in Cuba. Located 20 miles southwest of Miami, near the southern tip of Florida, Homestead AFB was in an ideal location to protect the southeast United States from attack by Cuba based aircraft. Beginning in 1967, twenty-six F-104As belonging to the 319th FIS received the more powerful J79-GE-19 engine. Following the deactivation of the 331st FIS at Webb AFB in February 1967, the 319th FIS became the final active duty Air Force squadron operating the F-104A until it was likewise disbanded in December 1969.[37]

After their withdrawal from active units, the Air Force had 24 F-104As converted into target drones.[38] This took place between 1960 and 1961 and resulted in these aircraft being redesignated as QF-104As. Following conversion, most of these drones received a high-visibility orange paint scheme. In such a configuration, QF-104As could be flown either as a piloted aircraft or by remote control depending upon the purpose of the mission. During its operational career, the QF-104A was operated primarily by the 3205th Drone Squadron at Eglin AFB. In 1972, QF-104A operations concluded after no less than twenty of these drones had been destroyed as aerial targets.

During 1963, three F-104As previously held in storage at Davis-Monthan AFB were converted into aerospace training aircraft and redesignated as NF-104As. During the conversion process, a 6,000 pound thrust Rocketdyne LR121-NA-1 (AR2-3) liquid fuel rocket engine was installed just above the tailpipe. Further modifications included the installation of a Reaction Control System (RCS), an enlarged fin, longer inlet shock cones, and a four-foot extension of the wingspan. The first two NF-104As were accepted by the Air Force during October 1963, while a third aircraft was delivered the following month. With the added thrust of their auxiliary rocket motors, NF-104As were able to reach extreme altitudes during a flight profile known as a zoom-climb. Shortly after entering service, the first NF-104A (56-0756) reached an altitude of 118,860 feet, setting an unofficial world altitude record. This achievement was surpassed on

An F-104C (56-0914) at the National Museum of the US Air Force in Dayton, Ohio. Note the aerial refueling probe extending alongside the left side of the cockpit and the gun port for the M61A1 cannon. (USAF)

December 6, 1963 when the same aircraft, piloted by Major R. W. Smith, was flown to altitude of 120,800 feet. Two NF-104As were written off during the type's operational career. The first accident occurred on December 10, 1963, when the third NF-104A (56-0762) went out of control at 104,000 feet and fell into a flat spin. The pilot, Colonel Charles E. "Chuck" Yeager, was able to eject from the aircraft at an altitude of approximately 8,000 feet, suffering serious injuries in the process. In June 1971, the first NF-104A experienced an inflight rocket motor explosion, and while the stricken aircraft was safely recovered, it was subsequently scrapped. Following the program's termination in December 1971, the second NF-104A (56-0760) was put on display at Edwards Air Force Base, where it remains to this day.

In July 1958, a multi-mission version of the Starfighter, the F-104C, took to the air for the first time. Although very similar to the F-104A, the F-104C was equipped with the more powerful General Electric J79-GE-7 engine that was capable of generating 15,800 pounds of thrust with afterburning.[39] The Tactical Air Command began receiving the C model during September 1958, with deliveries of the 77 examples built continuing through June of the following year. Four squadrons belonging to the 479th TFW were the sole operators of this version of the Starfighter, their transition from the F-100 Super Sabre having been completed during 1959.[40]

The F-104C retained the M61 Vulcan cannon that was common in the A model, this later being replaced by the improved M61A1. Besides the wingtip stations which could carry either 165-gallon external fuel tanks or AIM-9B Sidewinders, the F-104C was equipped with three additional pylons. Two of which were under the stubby trapezoidal wings, while a single pylon was located on the aircraft's centerline. The wing stations allowed for the carriage of a pair of 200-gallon drop tanks, while a single Mk 28 nuclear weapon could be loaded on the centerline pylon for the nuclear strike role.[41]

For day and clear night operations, the F-104C was equipped with the AN/ASG-14T-2 fire control system that was an improved version of the type installed in the F-104A.[42] However, the F-104C still lacked an all-weather capability, a deficiency that would minimize its effectiveness as a fighter-bomber during any European conflict. The C model was fitted with an in-flight refueling probe that extended alongside the canopy from the left hand side of the aircraft's fuselage.

In common with the F-104A, the C model possessed an outstanding performance capability that few aircraft have ever been able to equal, while even fewer have surpassed. On December 14, 1959, an F-104C piloted by Captain Joseph B. Jordan reached an altitude of 103,395 feet, thus becoming the first aircraft to exceed an altitude of 100,000 feet by taking off under its own power.

Beginning in October 1961, under Project Grindstone, the F-104C received the ability to carry an increased assortment of air-to-ground weapons, which included general-purpose bombs, napalm, and unguided rockets. At the same time, a new weapon mount became available that was capable of carrying an additional pair of Sidewinder missiles. This attached to the underside of the F-104C behind the nosewheel doors, but prevented the carrying of a nuclear device while in use. On an operational level, this device was somewhat frowned upon as its location made the sensitive seeker heads of the Sidewinders susceptible to damage from debris kicked up during takeoff or landing.

The USAF procured a two-seat training version of the F-104C designated as the F-104D, of which Lockheed delivered 21 examples between November 1958 and September 1959. Although the M61 cannon was deleted in this model, it retained an identical external stores capability as that found in the F-104C. As was the case with previous models of the Starfighter, the F-104C/D also experienced a poor safety record. During one five-year period (1959-1964), for example, twenty-four F-104C/Ds

The F-104D was a trainer version of the F-104C. As was the case with the F-104B, this model was not equipped with a M61A1 cannon. (USAF)

were destroyed in accidents, causing the deaths of nine Starfighter pilots. The number of aircraft lost represents nearly one-quarter of the total F-104C/Ds built and does not take into account at least 16 other major accidents during the same timeframe that did not result in aircraft being written off. To correct some of the reliability problems associated with J79-GE-7A, General Electric began upgrading the engine in May 1963 during Project Seven Up, a process that continued until June of the following year.[43]

In April 1965, F-104Cs from the 476th TFS began arriving at Kung Kuan AB in Taiwan following their deployment to Southeast Asia (SEA). Twenty-four F-104Cs in total would arrive in Taiwan, after which they began regular rotations to Da Nang AB in South Vietnam. The deployment of the Starfighter to Southeast Asia was in response to an urgent need to protect American attack aircraft as Operation Rolling Thunder increased the number of bombing sorties over North Vietnam. Apart from escorting strike packages, the F-104C also provided protection for USAF EC-121D Warning Star AEW (Airborne Early Warning) aircraft belonging to the 552nd Airborne Early Warning and Control Wing on deployment from McClellan AFB. The EC-121D, a militarized version of Lockheed's Super Constellation civil transport, arrived in SEA following the formation of the Big Eye Task Force in an effort to increase the radar coverage available to US commanders.[44] Among the duties performed by the crews of Big Eye EC-121Ds was the issuing of warnings to friendly aircraft about to trespass over the People's Republic of China.

In July 1965, the 436th TFS arrived in South Vietnam and assumed the duties previously assigned to the 476th TFS. During their deployment, F-104Cs belonging to the 476th TFS had only encountered enemy aircraft on two occasions, neither of which resulted in combat. Although serving primarily as an air defense fighter, the F-104C was often tasked with close air support and ground attack missions. During air-to-ground operations, Starfighter pilots earned a reputation for accuracy and quick reaction times, however, the F-104C's inadequate payload limited the type's usefulness as a fighter-bomber in Southeast Asia.

By the time that the 436th TFS's deployment concluded in October 1965, it had suffered four F-104C losses, three of which occurred on September 20, 1965 alone. On that date, Major Philip E. Smith was piloting an F-104C when he became lost over the Gulf of Tonkin. Under normal circumstances, a Big Eye EC-121D would have been on station to warn Smith that he was about to violate Chinese airspace. However, this incident occurred while the EC-121Ds were still on the ground at Tan Son Nhut. With no Big Eye aircraft on station to monitor his progress, Major Smith received no warning as he strayed into PRC airspace.[45] Shortly afterwards, a pair of Chinese J-6 (MiG-19)

A pair of F-104As (56-0769 & 56-0781) escorts a Lockheed EC-121 (55-0127) AEW aircraft. While deployed to SEA, F-104Cs were tasked with similar duties. (USAF)

jet fighters intercepted and shot down Smith's F-104C over Hainan Island. Following his capture by the PRC, Major Smith remained imprisoned until his release in March 1973. Troubles for the 436th TFS on that September day did not end with the downing of Smith's Starfighter, however, as two other F-104Cs assigned to a search mission for the missing plane were lost in a collision while approaching Da Nang. In this case, both pilots were rescued after successfully ejecting from their stricken aircraft.

On October 14, 1965, the 435th TFS replaced the 436th TFS at Da Nang. The operations of this squadron's F-104Cs were focused primarily on the escort role, particularly in protecting EC -121D surveillance aircraft over the Gulf of Tonkin. The 435th TFS's deployment was to be short-lived, however, as it departed Da Nang on 21 November bound for Kung Kuan, and eventually back to George AFB.

After a seven-month hiatus, the 435th TFS returned to Southeast Asia on June 6, 1966 when eight of its F-104Cs arrived at Udorn RTAFB, Thailand, to begin a deployment that lasted until July of the following year.[46] This movement was in response to the appearance of the MiG-21 over North Vietnam during the early months of 1966, which called US air superiority into question. Upon their deployment to Thailand, F-104Cs belonging to the 435th TFS were attached to the PACAF's 8th TFW.

The newly arrived Starfighters began flying escort for F-105 Thunderchiefs on strike missions over North Vietnam on June 7, 1966, just one day following their arrival in theater. As their aircraft were not fitted with any RHAWS gear, F-104C pilots were forced to rely upon the F-105s they were escorting for SAM warnings. Later, 435th TFS F-104Cs also provided protection for Wild Weasel missions over the North.

On July 22, 1966, the number of F-104Cs based at Udorn was

boosted by the arrival of twelve additional aircraft. During a one -hour period on August 1, 1966, two F-104Cs were shot down by North Vietnamese SAMs resulting in the deaths of their pilots. This led to the decision to withdraw the F-104C as an escort for strike missions over North Vietnam as it was considered that such assignments had become too dangerous for an aircraft without ECM gear. Later that month, F-104Cs shifted to the ground attack role in missions over Laos and South Vietnam.

Between September 1 and October 20, 1966, three Starfighters were lost during ground attack and armed reconnaissance missions.[47] During late 1966, under Project Pronto, all of the F-104Cs deployed to Southeast Asia received APR-25/26 RHAW gear. This modification, along with the questionable suitability of the Starfighter as a ground attack platform, led to the F-104C once again assigned to escort missions over the North beginning in December 1966. The F-104C operated out of Udorn until July 19, 1967 when it was withdrawn from SEA, being replaced by the F-4D Phantom II.

While the F-104C never downed an enemy aircraft during the Vietnam War, the true impact of the Starfighter upon the air war over Southeast Asia can be measured by its ability to deter aggression by North Vietnamese MiG fighters. Attesting to this was the fact that during F-104C deployments to SEA, a corresponding decrease in enemy fighter activity occurred. During its deployment history to Southeast Asia, fourteen F-104Cs were lost, eight to hostile fire and six to operational causes.

In 1967, the last F-104C/Ds were phased out of active-duty USAF squadrons and transferred to the 198th TFS of the Puerto Rico Air National Guard. For the 198th TFS, the F-104C/D represented a significant improvement in performance compared to the F-86H Sabre that it replaced. This squadron operated the Starfighter until July of 1975 when it transitioned to the A-7D Corsair II.

By 1957, it had become obvious to Lockheed that the US Air Force would acquire the F-104 in considerably smaller numbers than originally projected. Including the two XF-104 prototypes, the total USAF procurement of the Starfighter would amount to just 296 examples consisting of a mix of A, B, C, and D models. As such, the Starfighter has the distinction of being the Air Force's least acquired Century Series fighter. Although it appeared that the production history of the F-104 was about to come to a premature end, a significant reversal of fortunes for Lockheed was about to take place.

During the mid-1950s, several European NATO member nations began considering the purchase of a new supersonic fighter-bomber. Of this group, the largest customer was the Federal Republic of Germany (FRG), which was looking for a replacement for its Canadair Mk.5/6 Sabres and Republic F-84F Thunderstreaks.[48] As part of an effort to revitalize its aviation industry, West Germany intended to build a large portion of its aircraft under license.[49] The assumption that the winner of the competition for the NATO's next standard fighter-bomber could anticipate sales in excess of 1,000 aircraft elicited a number of proposals from aircraft manufacturers in England, France, Sweden, and the United States.

Lockheed's F-104G (Model 683-10-19) was an upgraded version of the Starfighter that was intended to serve as an all-weather multirole fighter-bomber. This represented a significant change in roles for an aircraft that had been originally designed as an air-superiority day fighter. As such, the F-104G was up against some serious competition which included, among others, the Republic F-105 Thunderchief and the Dassault Mirage III. Perhaps due to its notorious accident rate and the fact that USAF had purchased the F-104 only in limited numbers, it came as a surprise to many when the German government announced their selection of the F-104G in February 1959.

Externally, the F-104G differed little in appearance from the F-104C, nonetheless, it incorporated an extensive structural redesign. To manufacture the F-104G, Lockheed developed 36 new heavy-press forgings as well as numerous redesigned machined components and skin panels.[50] Compared to the F-104C, the structure of the F-104G received extra strengthening to permit the aircraft to operate more effectively at low altitudes. In common with the dual-place F-104B and D models, the F-104G featured an enlarged vertical fin to improve directional stability at high speed. In an effort to improve control during low-altitude operations at increased gross weights, the tailplane was given an increased hinge movement.[51]

Powering the F-104G was the General Electric J79-GE-11A turbojet which had a maximum thrust of 15,800 pounds with afterburning.[52] This engine had the same thrust capabilities as the J79-GE-7 turbojet, but incorporated additional reliability features.[53] To prevent ice build up, each of the engine inlets were equipped with a Spraymat electrical deicing system. The F-104G was fitted with an anti-skid braking system as well as an arrestor

A Luftwaffe F-104G stationed at Luke AFB during 1969. This model was the most numerous built version of the Starfighter, and as can be seen here, it incorporated a larger tail than the A and C models. (USAF)

hook under its tail section to prevent a runway overshoot.

Fitted into the F-104G's needle-like nose was the Autonetics F-15A North American Search and Ranging Radar (NASARR), which had both air-to-air and air-to-ground modes. This was an extremely advanced radar system for its day and provided airborne target detection and tracking information as well as ground mapping for accurate all-weather bombing. The F-104G was touted as being the first operational jet fighter in the world to be equipped with an inertial navigation system (INS) when it entered service with the Litton LN-3. Minneapolis-Honeywell produced the autopilot for the F-104G that enabled the pilot to select a constant indicated airspeed (IAS), heading, or rate of turn.[54]

The Federal Republic of Germany signed a contract with Lockheed on March 18, 1959 for the continued development of the F-104G and its ensuing manufacture under license in Germany.[55] Following Germany's selection of the F-104G, four additional NATO nations also entered into agreements to manufacture the Starfighter, these being Belgium, Canada, Italy, and the Netherlands.

In Europe, four consortiums undertook production of F-104G. Arge Süd consisted of the German firms Dornier, Heinkel, Messerschmitt, and Siebel, while Arge Nord members included Focke-Wulf, Hamburger Flugzeugbau, Weser Flugzeugbau, and the Dutch firms Aviolanda and Fokker. In Belgium, a western group was comprised of Avions Fairey and SABCA. Meanwhile, Aerfer, Fiat, Macchi, Piaggio, SACA, and SIAI-Marchetti formed a separate Italian Group.[56]

The F-104G flew for the first time at Palmdale, California on October 5, 1960. In May 1961, Lockheed delivered the first of 96 F-104Gs that it would build for the FRG. Meanwhile, license production in Europe was beginning with the first flight of an Arge Süd built F-104G taking place on August 10, 1961. This was followed by the maiden flight of a Starfighter manufactured by the Arge Nord group on November 11, 1961.[57] Several nations would acquire the Starfighter through US sponsored Military Assistance Programs (MAP).

In common with the F-104A and C, the F-104G was equipped with a M61 Vulcan cannon, while also retaining the standard option of carrying either a pair of AIM-9 Sidewinders or drop tanks on its wingtip stations. The type's air interception capability was enhanced by the option of carrying two further Sidewinders mounted on the bottom of the fuselage behind the nose gear doors. For air-to-ground operations, the F-104G was capable of carrying a 2,000 pound payload on its centerline pylon, while an additional 1,000 pounds worth of ordinance could be mounted under each wing.[58]

The F-104G represented a formidable strike aircraft when it

This view illustrates the external stores load capability of the F-104G. (USAF)

entered service in Europe during the early 1960s. Given its capability of reaching a speed of nearly Mach 1 at sea level, combined with a small radar signature, the F-104G would have been a difficult target for any Warsaw Pact forces attempting to stop it. The F-104G performance capabilities also made it an ideal candidate as a dedicated tactical reconnaissance platform. This directly led to the development of the RF-104G which could carry three KS-67A 70mm still picture cameras inside of its fuselage instead of the M61 Vulcan cannon. Initial operators of the RF-104G, of which 194 were built, included Germany's Luftwaffe and the Netherland's Koninklijke Luchtmacht.[59]

In order to begin training German instructor pilots prior to the start of F-104G deliveries, it was decided to develop a two-seat version of the Starfighter for the Luftwaffe. Designated as the F-104F, Lockheed built 30 examples of this variant, the first of which was delivered in October 1959. Derived from the F-104D, the F-104F lacked the all-weather NASARR radar found in the F-104G, and was not considered to be combat capable. Later, the dual-place TF-104G was developed which possessed a combat capability similar to the F-104G, leading to the withdrawal of the F-104F from Luftwaffe service in 1971.

In order to accommodate the second cockpit, the TF-104G was not equipped with a M61 Vulcan cannon and featured a reduced internal fuel load compared to the F-104G. Although the TF-104G was outfitted with similar avionics and able to carry much the same weapons employed by the single-seat model, it lacked a centerline pylon. Lockheed manufactured all of the 220 TF-104Gs built, with 48 of these being constructed using consortium supplied components.

Besides the four European nations participating in consortium manufacturing agreements, five other NATO members procured new-build Starfighters for their air forces. This group consisted of Denmark, Greece, Norway, Spain, and Turkey, which

To assist in the training of their pilots in the United States, several German F-104Gs were based at Luke AFB, Arizona. Although receiving USAF markings, these aircraft were the property of the Federal Republic of Germany. Here is a F-104G from the 69th Tactical Fighter Training Squadron. (DI)

obtained their T/F-104Gs from Lockheed and Canadair, using MAP funds. In total, Canadair manufactured 140 F-104Gs under license for such programs. When production of the single-seat F-104G concluded in 1973, no less than 1,122 examples of the type had been built, a number that equates to nearly four times the number of all F-104s, of various models, purchased by the USAF.

Airspace restrictions combined with the generally poor weather conditions in Europe prompted the Federal Republic of Germany to request assistance from the USAF in meeting its F-104 pilot training needs. The Air Force responded by entering into a Military Assistance Training Program (MATP) agreement to train FRG pilots at the Tactical Air Command's F-104 combat crew training course at Luke AFB, Arizona.[60] Beginning in 1964 and ending in 1982 a number of FRG T/F-104Gs were assigned to Luke AFB to be used by the student pilots and their USAF instructors. Although these aircraft received USAF serial numbers and markings, they remained the property of the FRG. Besides German pilots, a number of their counterparts from other nations supplied F-104s through MAP programs also received training at Luke AFB. This included pilots from Denmark, Greece, Norway, Spain, and Turkey.

The poor safety record that had dogged the F-104 since its earliest days followed it into service with the Luftwaffe and the air arm of the German Navy, the Marineflieger. Shorty after becoming operational, the F-104G was involved in a number of controversial crashes, which generated a wave of public criticism concerning the German government's decision to acquire the Starfighter. While possessing truly impressive performance capabilities, the Starfighter was a tricky aircraft to fly, one that would rarely forgive even the smallest of mistakes. This characteristic combined with the inherit dangers associated with the low-level operations that the F-104G was conducting in Europe's tumultuous weather led to a large percentage of these accidents. The frequency of Luftwaffe F-104G crashes grew so quickly that by 1962 the type was suffering a loss rate of 139 per 100,000 hours, with many of the losses resulting in pilot fatalities.[61]

The excessive loss rate experienced by Germany's F-104 fleet led to the type receiving a number of uncomplimentary nicknames in that nation. Among these were Fliegender Sarg (Flying Coffin), Erdnagel (Ground Nail), and the Witwenmacher (Widow Maker). Out of the 916 Starfighters acquired by Germany, 292 were lost in crashes, killing 115 pilots.[62]

In an effort to improve pilot survivability, Luftwaffe officials began a campaign to have the F-104G's Lockheed C-2 ejection seat replaced by a Martin-Baker seat. Previously, the Luftwaffe had experienced a major improvement in reliability and pilot survivability after fitting Martin-Baker seats to their Canadair Sabres and F-84F Thunderstreaks. However, there was opposition to such a move by certain establishments in the United States that prevented final approval to equip the F-104G with a Martin-Baker ejection seat until March 8, 1967. Within a year's time, both Italy and Germany had retrofitted their entire fleets of F-104s with the Martin-Baker GQ-7 ejection seat.[63]

The Starfighter remained in frontline duty with the Luftwaffe and Marineflieger throughout the 1970s and into the early 80s prior to being retired following the arrival of the Panavia Tornado. In the event of war breaking out between NATO and the Warsaw Pact during this period, Marineflieger F-104Gs would have been tasked with anti-shipping operations in the Baltic. To perform this mission, the F-104G would have been outfitted with the Kormoran anti-ship missile.[64]

During its operational career, the F-104G was involved in numerous German aeronautical research projects, including Zero -Length Launch (ZEL) trials. As described in Chapter 1, the ZEL process enabled a tactical jet fighter armed with a nuclear weapon to be launched from a standstill using a solid rocket motor in the event that an enemy attack managed to render an airbase's runways inoperable. Initial ZEL tests involving a Luftwaffe F-104G took place at Edwards Air Force Base in 1963. Later testing, involving two F-104Gs were conducted in Germany before the project was abandoned during the late 1960s.

The F-104G was retired from the German Luftwaffe in 1987. By that time, a number of other European operators had also phased out their F-104G Starfighters, with many of these going to other operators such as Turkey and Taiwan. In 1972, Spain traded in its F-104Gs for the F-4C. Between 1979 and 1986, the F-104G was replaced by the F-16 Fighting Falcon in the air forces of Belgium, Denmark, Norway, and the Netherlands. Meanwhile, Greece continued operating its F-104Gs until 1993 before finally replacing the type with the A-7E Corsair II.

On September 17, 1959, the Canadian government signed a licensing agreement with Lockheed to build a version of the F-

104G specifically tailored to the needs of the Royal Canadian Air Force (RCAF) designated as the CF-104. Chosen to manufacture this variant of the Starfighter was Canadair Ltd. of Montreal. This firm was no stranger to such manufacturing arrangements in that it had previously built versions of the North American F-86 Sabre and Lockheed's T-33 Shooting Star under license. To serve as a pattern, Lockheed delivered a single F-104A to Canadair prior to the fabrication of the first CF-104. Unlike the multi-role F-104G, however, the CF-104 was configured primarily for the nuclear strike role, although it was able to carry a Vicom camera pod fitted with four 70mm Vinten cameras to perform photoreconnaissance duties. It also differed in that it had R-24A NASARR equipment installed, which unlike the F-104G's F15A NASARR was optimized to operate in an air-to-ground mode.[65] The CF-104 was originally equipped with Litton's LN-3 INS, which during the later years of its career was replaced by the more capable LW-33 INS.

An overhead shot of a CF-104. When this aircraft first entered service with the RCAF, it was primarily tasked with the nuclear strike role in Europe. (CF)

The first two CF-104s built by Canadair were shipped to Lockheed's Palmdale facility, where the first of these aircraft took to the air on May 26, 1961. This was followed on August 14, 1961 by the first flights in Canada of the third and fourth Starfighter built by Canadair.[66] Powering the CF-104 was a licensed version of General Electric's J79 engine built by Orenda Engines Ltd., which was designated as the J79-OEL-7. Besides the 200 CF-104s it built for the RCAF, Canadair also built 140 F-104Gs under the MAP program for European users.

By 1972, Canada's fleet of CF-104s had received modifications enabling them to perform in the conventional attack role as the emphasis of their operations shifted away from nuclear strike duties. This included the installation of a M61A1 Vulcan cannon, which had been omitted from the CF-104's original weapons fit, and bomb ejector racks.

At the same time that it entered into the CF-104 manufacturing agreement, the Canadian government also placed an order with Lockheed to acquire a two-seat version of the aircraft designated as the CF-104D. This variant was to be built by Lockheed at Palmdale, with the type's first flight taking place on June 14, 1961. The original order for 14 aircraft was followed by two additional orders placed in October 1961 and November 1963 that brought the total procurement of the CF-104D to 38 examples.[67]

Beginning in 1983, the entry into service of the McDonnell Douglas CF-18 Hornet allowed Air Command to begin retiring its aging fleet of Starfighters.[68] This transition continued until March 1986, when the last active unit operating the type, the No. 441 Squadron, retired the last of its CF-104s. After their removal from the service, many of these aircraft were transferred to Turkey. As had been experienced by the Luftwaffe and Marineflieger, Canadian Starfighters also suffered a high loss rate while in operational service. It has been estimated that 110

An Italian F-104S is accompanied by a Italian Tornado, a two-seat Turkish TF-104G, and a USAF A-7D Corsair II participating in the NATO exercise Dragon Hammer '87. (DI)

out of the 238 CF-104/CF-104Ds built were lost in accidents.

During the mid-1960s, Italy's air force, the Aeronautica Militare Italiana (AMI), issued its AWX requirement calling for an all-weather fighter. After evaluating several different aircraft, including the McDonnell F-4 Phantom and the BAC Lightning during 1965, the AMI chose a derivative of Lockheed's F-104 Starfighter designated as the Model CL-980. This aircraft was to become the F-104S, the S signifying its compatibility with the Raytheon AIM-7 Sparrow SARH missile.[69]

On December 22, 1966, an Italian F-104G modified by Lockheed to F-104S specifications flew for the first time. Production of the F-104S, however, was to take place in Italy by Fiat (Aeritalia), with the first such example flying just over two years later on December 30, 1968. While the F-104S had many similarities to the F-104G, it was equipped with the more powerful J79-GE-19 turbojet that had an afterburning thrust rating of 17,900 pounds.

Unlike the F-104G, which was equipped with the Autonetics F -15A NASARR radar, the F-104S was fitted with a FIAR R-21G/H radar set.[70] This installation was capable of illuminating targets for the AIM-7 Sparrow missile, and while optimized for the air-to-air role, the R-21G/H also featured ground mapping and terrain avoidance modes. The F-104S was equipped with nine hardpoints on which a mix of air-to-air or air-to-ground weapons could be loaded. This included the wingtip stations, two pylons under each wing, twin pylons under the fuselage below the intakes, and a centerline station. Aircraft operating as fighter-bombers were equipped with the M61 Vulcan cannon, a feature that F-104Ss serving as interceptors lacked.

The F-104S entered service with the AMI during 1969. This air arm eventually acquired 205 examples, while the Turkish Air Force, the Türk Hava Kuvvetleri, received 40 additional F-104Ss before production ended in 1979.[71] The delivery of the final F-104S also marked the end of worldwide Starfighter production, some twenty-five years following the type's maiden flight.

Beginning in 1986, the AMI commenced upgrading 147 of their F-104Ss to the F-104S ASA (Aggiornamento Sistema d'Arma, or Weapons System Updating) specification. This included the installation of the FIAR R-21G/M1 Setter radar that possessed a true look-down/shoot-down capability and compatibility with the Selenia Aspide 1A medium range SARH AAM. Further enhancements included the fitting of a new weapons delivery computer, improved ECM gear, and a new IFF system. The incorporation of new miniaturized electronic gear allowed the installation of the M61 Vulcan cannon. Aircraft upgraded to the F-104S-ASA standard were also capable of carrying the all-aspect AIM-9L Sidewinder IR AAM.

During the 1990s, significant delays experienced by the Eurofighter program led to the AMI's decision to extend the service life its Starfighters through the rebuilding of 49 F-104S ASAs and 15 TF-104Gs to the ASA-M standard. The modernization process included the replacement of several structural components, installation of a GPS system, updated cockpit displays, and a new Litton LN-30A2 INS. Delivery of the first F-104S ASA-M took place in late 1998 when the 23° Gruppo of 5° Stormo received their first upgraded Starfighter. The F-104 remained in service with the AMI until its retirement in October 2004. This signified not only the end of the Starfighter's long career with Italy's air force, but also the end of its active military service worldwide.

Another large user of the F-104 was Japan, which signed a licensing agreement to build the Starfighter on January 29, 1960.[72] Designated as the F-104J, this version flew for the first time on June 30, 1961. The F-104J was similar to the F-104G but was dedicated to the air intercept role rather than air-to-ground operations due to treaty restrictions placed upon the exporting of aircraft with offensive capabilities to Japan.

Lockheed built the first three F-104Js that were later broken down and shipped to Japan for reassembly by Mitsubishi.[73] Following this, Lockheed shipped twenty-nine additional F-104Js in kit form to Japan for final assembly. Besides these initial aircraft, Mitsubishi manufactured an additional 178 F-104Js for the Japan Air Self-Defense Force (JASDF) before production ceased in 1967. During this timeframe, the JASDF also acquired twenty F-104DJ two-seat trainers directly from Lockheed.

To power the F-104J, Ishikawajima-Harima Heavy Industries manufactured a licensed version of the J79 engine designated as the J79-IHI-11A. The F-104J was equipped with the NASARR F-15J-31 radar and armed with an internal M61 Vulcan cannon and up to four AIM-9 Sidewinder AAMs. During its time in service with the JASDF, the F-104J earned the nickname "Eikou" (Glory).[74] The Starfighter served with the JASDF until

F-104Js belonging to the Japan Air Self-Defense Force (JASDF) F-104Js on the flight line during the early 1980s. (DI)

being supplanted by the McDonnell Douglas F-15J Eagle during the early 1980s, with the last F-104J being retired in 1986.

A number of air forces around the world operated F-104s after acquiring them second-hand from other operators. In 1961, Pakistan received a small number of ex-USAF Starfighters under MAP. This transaction involved 10 F-104As and 2 F-104Bs, which was followed by a further transfer of two additional F-104As during 1964-65. Although exact numbers are unclear, the Republic of China (Taiwan) received at least 25 F-104As and 2 F-104Bs directly from the United States between 1960 and 1961. Later, as they became available, the ROCAF also secured a significant number of second-hand Starfighters of various types from Belgium, Denmark, Germany, and Japan before retiring the type in 1998. In early 1967, Jordan received 2 F-104As and 3 F-104Bs directly from the United States. Just prior to the outbreak of the Six Day War in June 1967, these aircraft were flown to Turkey where they sat out the conflict between Israel and its

Arab neighbors.[75] As a consequence of the Six Day War, further F
-104 deliveries to Jordan were delayed before resuming during
1969. In total, 29 F-104As and 4 two-seat F-104Bs were delivered
to the Royal Jordanian Air Force, which operated the Starfighter
until 1983. Turkey became another large customer in the market
for used Starfighters by acquiring surplus aircraft from Belgium,
Canada, Germany, Norway, and the Netherlands. The
Starfighter served with the Türk Hava Kuvvetleri until being
phased out in June 1994.

Other than its service with the USAF during the Vietnam War,
the F-104 was involved in relatively few combat operations
during its lengthy operational career. This is truly remarkable
given the aircraft's widespread use in air forces that spanned the
globe. Despite this, however, the Starfighter was involved in two
separate conflicts between India and Pakistan and at least one
aerial engagement between Taiwan and the People's Republic of
China during its period of service.

During the 1965 Indo-Pakistani War, there existed the
possibility of a match-up between Pakistan's F-104A/B
interceptors and its chief Soviet-built rival, the MiG-21 operated
by India. In the end, such an engagement did not occur as
India's small force of MiG-21s were used in only a few
operational missions.[76] On September 3, 1965, three days after
Pakistani troops marched into Indian Kashmir, a Pakistan Air
Force (PAF) F-104 forced an Indian Gnat to land at the Pasrur
airfield where both the aircraft and its pilot were quickly
captured. On 6 September, another PAF Starfighter succeeded in
downing an Indian Air Force (IAF) Dassault Mystére IVA with a
Sidewinder missile. The following day, a flight of six IAF
Mystéres attacked the Sargodha airbase during which a lone
Pakistani F-104 was able to knock down one of the attackers with
its cannon. Shortly afterwards, however, the Starfighter was
itself shot down after getting into a dogfight with the remaining

Mystéres.[77] On the night of 21 September, a PAF F-104 piloted by Squadron Leader Jamal A. Khan brought down an IAF Canberra with a AIM-9 Sidewinder after intercepting the British-built jet bomber at 33,000 feet. On September 22, 1965, both India and Pakistan agreed to accept an UN-sponsored cease-fire agreement.

A little more than six years later, war again broke out between India and Pakistan on December 3, 1971 when the PAF made preemptive strikes against Indian airfields and military installations. By this time, Pakistan only had one operational squadron of F-104A/Bs consisting of just seven aircraft. Meanwhile, India had greatly increased its inventory of MiG-21s since the 1965 war and had no less than eight squadrons available at the beginning of hostilities.[78] During the ensuing conflict, Pakistan's meager Starfighter force of was reinforced by 10 F-104s sent from Jordan. On December 10, 1971, a PAF F-104 downed an Indian Navy Alizé over the Arabian Sea off the coast of Karachi, Pakistan.

Although both sides have widely varying accounts of their respective aerial victories and losses, it appears that there were at least two engagements between PAF F-104s and IAF MiG-21s during the war. The first occurred on 12 December when a pair of MiG-21FLs engaged an F-104 that had just strafed Jamnagar airfield. One of Indian MiG-21s fired a K-13 IR (AA-2 Atoll) missile at the fleeing Starfighter, which missed.[79] Failing to hit the PAF F-104 with a missile, the Indian pilot closed the distance and downed the Starfighter with cannon fire. The second occurred on the last day of the war, December 17, 1971, when a IAF MiG-21 reportedly shot down a PAF F-104 that was flying cover for a flight of F-86 Sabres near Naya Chor.[80]

On the afternoon of January 13, 1967, four ROCAF F-104Gs engaged eight Shenyang J-6s (MiG-19s) belonging to the People's Liberation Army Air Force (PLAAF) near the island of Quemoy.

A NASA TF-104G (N824NA) flies in formation with a NB-52B during the DAST (Drones for Aerodynamic and Structural Testing) program. (NASA)

During the ensuing dogfight, a pair of F-104Gs each shot down a single J-6 using AIM-9 Sidewinders. One of the four Starfighters, however, failed to return to base, with the PLAAF claiming that its aircraft had brought down the missing F-104 while the ROCAF blamed the loss on a sudden mechanical or fuel malfunction.

On August 2, 1956, the seventh YF-104A (55-2961) was transferred to NACA (later NASA) for use in a variety of flight test programs. This organization would eventually acquire 11 examples of various single and dual-seat models of the Starfighter, including 3 F-104Gs obtained during 1963 that were redesignated as F-104Ns. One of these F-104Ns was lost on June 8, 1966 when it collided with a North American XB-70A Valkyrie supersonic bomber prototype during a photographic mission. The collision and subsequent crash of both aircraft caused the death of the F-104N's pilot, Joe Walker, and the copilot of the XB-

70A, Major Carl S. Cross. Among the projects in which the Starfighter participated in while employed by NASA was roll coupling research, reaction control system testing, and Space Shuttle thermal protection tile durability. NASA continued operating the F-104 Starfighter until its retirement in February 1994, following a long and successful career.

The last chapter of the Starfighter's involvement with NASA has yet to be written, however, as F-104s belonging to Starfighters, Inc. began flight operations from the Shuttle Landing Facility (SLF) at Cape Kennedy, Florida in April 2007. Starfighters, Inc. was formed during the early 1990s by acquiring second-hand F-104s from foreign sources to perform aerial demonstrations at air shows throughout the United States. Headquartered at the John F. Kennedy Space Center, Florida, the primary focus of this company has since shifted to performing government contract work. In May 2011, NASA announced that F-104s belonging to Starfighters, Inc. would be involved in a program to launch nanosatellites using 19-foot long rockets that would be deployed at an altitude of 60,000-feet.[81]

During the 1960s, Lockheed proposed a number of improved versions of the F-104, including the CL-1200 Lancer, which it entered into the International Fighter Aircraft (IFA) competition. The CL-1200 was developed from the F-104G, but incorporated shoulder mounted wings and a completely redesigned rear fuselage with low mounted tailplanes. In November 1970, the CL-1200 lost out to the Northrop F-5E Tiger II in the IFA competition. Lockheed, however, continued to promote its design to the USAF. At the time, the Air Force was in the midst of the F-15 program and fearing that the CL-1200 could possibly divert funding from the McDonnell Douglas air-superiority fighter prompted Lockheed's design to be assigned the experimental X-27 designation in April 1971.[82] Revisions to the CL-1200 design included a larger wing, redesigned fin, and rectangular air intakes. With the Air Force considering the procurement of at least one aircraft for research purposes, Lockheed constructed a full-scale mock-up. In the end, however, the USAF decided not to purchase any X-27s and the project came to an end. The CL-1200-2 was a further revised version of the X-27 that Lockheed entered into the USAF's Lightweight Fighter Competition. In 1972, the CL-1200-2 was removed from consideration in the competition when General Dynamics and Northrop were awarded contracts to build prototypes of their design proposals designated as the YF-16 and YF-17 respectively. Following this, Lockheed made an unsuccessful attempt to promote the CL-1200-2 abroad in the export market before finally abandoning the project in 1973.

Despite the fact that it was purchased in only limited quantities by the air force for which it had been developed, the F-104 later evolved into becoming one of Europe's premier tactical fighter-bombers, a role it fulfilled for nearly a quarter of a century. Despite its idiosyncrasies, many of which could lead to fatal results, a great many of the pilots who flew the Starfighter praised its capabilities. With its pointed features making it appear to be going a thousand miles-an-hour just sitting on the ground, there can be little wonder as to why the F-104 Starfighter has become one of the most iconic aircraft of the Cold War era.

# Chapter Five
## Republic F-105 Thunderchief

In 1936, the Seversky Aircraft Corporation's SEV-1XP monoplane beat out competing designs from Consolidated, Curtiss, and Vought to win a United States Army Air Corps (USAAC) competition for a pursuit fighter.[1] This aircraft was to become the USAAC's first operational single-seat, all-metal, pursuit plane equipped with a retractable landing gear. Located at Farmingdale, New York, Seversky Aircraft received a production contract from the Army for 77 examples of this fighter designated as the P-35. Seversky also managed to sell 120 additional aircraft, designated as EP-1s (EP-106s), to Sweden, 60 of which were later requisitioned in October 1940 by the US Government and placed into Army service as P-35As.[2] The designer of the P-35 was Alexander Kartveli whom had arrived in the United States during 1928 after working in France for a number of years. Born in 1896 at Tiflis (Tbilisi), Georgia, Kartveli became the Seversky Aircraft Corporation's chief engineer in 1931.

Although it never served in substantial numbers, the P-35 paved the way for Kartveli to develop the P-43 Lancer that entered service in May 1941. By this time, the Seversky Aircraft Corporation had become the Republic Aviation Corporation following the 1939 ouster of Alexander de Seversky by its board of directors. The P-43 was powered by a 1,200-hp Pratt & Whitney R-1830 Twin Wasp radial engine equipped with a turbo

-supercharger and was capable of reaching a top speed of 349 mph.[3]

In November 1939, the USAAC awarded Republic a contract to construct a XP-47 prototype powered by a 1,150-hp Allison inline engine.[4] As Kartveli and his team worked on developing this aircraft, the results of early World War II air battles over Europe became available to aircraft designers in the United States. Realizing that a lack of heavy armor and self-sealing fuel tanks made their current design unsuitable for the evolving nature of aerial warfare, Republic submitted a revised proposal to the USAAC in June 1940 for a larger and more heavily armed aircraft. This called for a fighter powered by a 2,000-hp Pratt & Whitney R-2800 Double Wasp engine and armed with eight .50 caliber machine guns. After reviewing the revamped design, the USAAC gave Republic approval to proceed with the P-47B in September 1940. Named the Thunderbolt, initial deliveries of production P-47Bs to 56th Fighter Group began in June 1942. The P-47 would go on to become one of the great Allied fighter-bombers of the Second World War.

During the final years of the war, the first jet fighters began taking to the skies. More than anything else, jet propulsion would shape postwar fighter aircraft development. Republic managed to capitalize on this technological shift with another of Kartveli's aircraft designs, the P-84 Thunderjet. The genesis of this design began in November 1944, after Republic had studied axial turbojet powered versions of its P-47 Thunderbolt.[5] The first flight of a Thunderjet took place on February 28, 1946 when the XP-84, thundered into the skies above Muroc Army Airfield, California.

The P-84 was later redesignated as the F-84 following the establishment of the US Air Force as a separate branch of the military in 1947. As was the case with most first-generation jets, the F-84 Thunderjet was equipped with straight wings. The F-84 went on to perform superlatively during the Korean War as a fighter-bomber, particularly in the low-level interdiction role. The Thunderjet, however, was inferior to the MiG-15 in the air-to -air arena. In an effort to increase the performance of its F-84 design, Republic created a significantly revised model designated as the F-84F Thunderstreak that incorporated a deeper fuselage, sweptback wings, and a more powerful Wright J65 engine. Although retaining the F-84 designation, the F-84F was largely a new aircraft. A further development of this aircraft was the RF-84F Thunderflash, which was a reconnaissance version of the Thunderstreak fitted with an enclosed nose section to house up to fifteen separate cameras. By necessity, the RF-84F featured inlets mounted on extended wing roots, in opposition to the nose intake ducts common with the rest of the F-84 family.

Although Republic was able to secure significant production contracts with the USAF, the F-84 also represented a considerable export success. As such, Republic supplied numerous examples to friendly nations around the globe, particularly in Europe where it served in the air forces of many NATO members. The most produced version of the F-84, the G model, was the first US Air Force fighter aircraft that was capable of delivering an atomic bomb against a target, a capability previously possessed only by large bomber aircraft.

During the early 1950s, Republic began studying a revised version of the F-84F that could carry a tactical nuclear weapon in an enclosed bomb bay rather than mounted externally. While such an arrangement was attainable from an engineering standpoint, the addition of the necessary equipment would have led to serious performance penalties given the aircraft's available power.[6] Concurrently, Alexander Kartveli's engineering team was working on an entirely new design powered by a General Electric J73 turbojet and designated as the AP-63. As their design evolved, engineers at Republic would replace the J73 powerplant with the Allison J71 turbojet.[7] Developed around the requirements of the nuclear strike role, the AP-63 design represented a large single-engine attack aircraft possessing a secondary air-to-air capability.

The development of a new fighter offered a significant increase in warfighting capability and performance compared to a revamped F-84 derivative. Among the advantages offered was the capability of the aircraft to reach supersonic speeds at low-altitude. During the development of the AP-63, Kartvelli's engineers had investigated no less than 108 different configurations for the aircraft.[8] In April 1952, Republic proposed the AP-63 (Manufacturers Model AP-63-31) to the Air Force, which approved the design in May of that year, preferring a completely new aircraft rather than a further development of the F-84F.[9]

In September 1952, the USAF issued a letter contract covering the engineering development, tooling design, and material procurement for an envisioned manufacture of 199 examples of Republic's fighter-bomber under the auspices of Weapon System 306A (WS-306A). By this time, the aircraft had been designated as the F-105 and was anticipated to enter service in 1955. During March 1953, however, the Air Force reduced their order to only 46 aircraft composed of 37 F-105s and 9 RF-105s.[10]

In an effort to reduce the time between the beginning of the program and the F-105's entry into operational service, its production plan utilized the Cook-Craigie plan. This was the same method used during the procurement of the F-102 Delta Dagger. As explained earlier, this type of approach relied heavily upon the assumption that there would be no significant problems with the basic design of the aircraft. If, however, subsequent testing revealed that substantial design changes were necessary, such an occurrence would likely lead to an expensive retooling of the production line along with corresponding modification programs to retrofit changes into aircraft already produced. The 1950s represented an era in aviation history in which fighter aircraft were becoming increasingly complex while at the same time engineers were making pioneering efforts into the unknown territory surrounding supersonic flight. As had been discovered during the F-102 program, unforeseen difficulties can greatly offset the advantages of utilizing the Cook -Craigie method of production.

In October 1953, Republic presented a full-scale engineering mock-up of the F-105 to the Air Force at Farmingdale. While no significant changes were recommended at the time, there was some discussion considering the use of the Pratt & Whitney J57 as an interim engine to address concerns that Allison's J71 might not be able meet the thrust requirements necessary for the F-105. At the time, deliveries of the first aircraft were anticipated to occur in the spring of 1955.[11]

Even though it had received an initial order from the USAF, Republic was to endure a long and twisting path on its journey to getting the F-105 into operational service. In December 1953, with Republic experiencing significant delays, the Air Force suspended the procurement of the F-105. In February of the following year, however, the Air Force reinstated the program while also reducing the number of F-105s ordered to only 15 aircraft. Prior to the Air Force's resumption of F-105 procurement, the growing weight of the aircraft had prompted the decision to switch its powerplant from the Allison J71 to the Pratt & Whitney J75 turbojet engine. To finance the changes necessary to fit their J75 engine into the aircraft, Pratt & Whitney was able to secure funding from the F-105 program.[12]

In September 1954, with the program continuing to suffer delays, the Air Force reduced their procurement further to just three F-105s. A month later, however, the Air Force revised their order once again, this time doubling it to six aircraft. On

December 1, 1954, some twenty-seven months following the issuance of its letter of contract to Republic, the Air Force issued General Operational Requirement 49 (GOR 49) to cover the specific characteristics of the F-105. Between December 1954 and April 1955, the USAF revised GOR 49 on three separate occasions. GOR 49 called for an inflight refueling capability, a complex fire control system, and improved performance.[13] In February 1955, the Air Force once again revised its procurement to 15 test aircraft, consisting of 2 YF-105As, 3 RF-105Bs, and 10 F-105Bs.

Powering the two YF-105As was the Pratt & Whitney J57-P-25 turbojet that had a rated thrust of 16,000 pounds with afterburning. This engine, of which only six were ever manufactured, was derived from the J57-P-21 used by the F-100 Super Sabre.[14] After being assembled in Republic's Farmingdale plant, the first YF-105A was broken down for shipment to Edwards AFB, where it would begin the test flight phase of the

The number one YF-105A (54-0098) at Edwards Air Force Base. (USAF)

146

program.

On October 22, 1955, the YF-105A flew for the first time with Republic's chief test pilot Russell "Rusty" Roth at the controls. During this forty-five minute flight, the YF-105A reached a speed of Mach 1.05 at 30,000 feet. Despite this achievement, however, the supersonic capability of the aircraft was hampered by transonic drag issues inherit to its design. Such an affliction was common during the early days of supersonic aircraft development, as can be witnessed by Convair's troubles with their F-102 Delta Dagger.

After accumulating only 22 hours of flight time, the short career of the first YF-105A ended on December 16, 1955. On that date, while this aircraft was traveling at approximately 530 knots the right main landing gear was ripped away after it deployed unexpectedly. Following the incident, Russell Roth was able to land the YF-102A at Edwards with its nose and left main gears still retracted. Although the YF-105A managed to remain relatively intact during the emergency wheels-up landing, the structural damage it received was sufficient to end its flying career.

The following month witnessed the first flight of the second YF-105A when it took to the skies on January 28, 1956. This plane differed from the first YF-105A in that it had a smooth exhaust nozzle, compared to the first aircraft that had a four-section petal system that became standard in the production version of the F-105. Capable of being extended outwards by as much as 90-degrees while in flight, the four petals of the exhaust section were able to function as airbrakes. To avoid the top petal from fouling the braking parachute and the bottom petal from striking the ground, only the two horizontal petal segments were available to slow the F-105 down during landing.

Wind tunnel testing conducted prior to the type's first flight found that the F-105A would not be capable of speeds much above Mach 1.0 due to excessive transonic drag. In a solution similar to that employed by Convair during the redesign of its F-102 Delta Dagger, the area rule principle pioneered by Richard T. Whitcomb was applied to the F-105 design in an effort to mitigate the drag issue.

With area ruling applied, the waist of the aircraft was pinched and the aft fuselage was bulged behind the wings. Using a 1/22-scale model of the YF-105A, NACA conducted wind tunnel tests to verify the improvements made by the design changes. Initially resisting making changes to his design, Alexander Kartveli sent an observer to witness the testing. After Kartveli was presented with the positive results from this experimentation, he agreed to incorporate the area rule principal into the F-105 design, but with a bulge at approximately 80 percent of the NACA recommendation.[15]

Besides the area rule alterations, other changes to the design included a taller vertical tail, longer forward fuselage, and revised engine inlets. The YF-105As featured an inlet design generally similar to that used by the RF-84F Thunderflash. However, beginning with the F-105B these were replaced by unique forward-swept intakes, giving the aircraft a unique planform. To supply the engine with the proper amount of air at all speeds, Republic engineers fitted the F-105 with a variable air inlet system. This arrangement worked by utilizing a set of movable cones inside of the inlet to change its cross-section, thereby controlling the amount of air being permitted to pass through to the engine.

Piloted by Republic's test pilot Henry Beaird, the first F-105B (54-0100) embarked on its maiden flight at Edwards AFB on May 26, 1956.[16] This flight proved uneventful until Beaird attempted to extend the undercarriage in preparation to bring the aircraft in for a landing. After selecting gear down, only the main undercarriage deployed with the nose gear remaining in the

The third pre-production F-105B (54-0102) is found at Edwards AFB on December 16, 1959. (NASA)

stowed position. Despite his best efforts, the nose gear refused to extend, thus forcing Beaird to make a belly landing on the desert floor. Since the Second World War, Republic Aviation had earned a distinction for producing some very strong aircraft. During the first F-105B's "wheels up" landing, this reputation was reinforced as the aircraft suffered only minimal damage. While it was being picked up from the desert floor, however, the aircraft sustained major airframe damage when an error made by a crane operator resulted in it being dropped from a short height.

Following Beaird's crash landing, undercarriage issues continued to plague the F-105B flight test program. On January 30, 1957, while flying the second F-105B, Republic test pilot Lindell "Lin" Hendrix was forced to perform a belly-landing when the main gear of his aircraft failed to deploy. While Hendrix was uninjured in the incident, the aircraft sustained significant damage to its fuselage. The fourth F-105B built also experienced a similar undercarriage malfunction.[17] A subsequent

149

investigation revealed that under certain conditions, the auxiliary air intakes inside of the wheel wells were opening while the main undercarriage was still retracted. During such an occurrence, the possibility existed that the suction created would be sufficient to prevent the gear from extending. A solution to this problem was found in the fitting of an interlock system to the auxiliary inlet system.[18]

Early production F-105Bs were powered by the 23,500 pound thrust Pratt & Whitney J75-P-5 afterburning turbojet engine. Beginning with the third production batch, subsequent F-105Bs received the more powerful J75-P-19 capable of generating an additional 1,000 pounds of thrust and giving the aircraft a top speed of 1386 mph (Mach 2.1) at 36,000 feet. Measuring 63 feet 1 inch in length, the F-105B was two feet longer than its predecessor, the YF-105A. Rounding out the F-105B's dimensions was its wingspan of 34 feet 11 inches and height of 19 feet 8 inches. Thus far, the F-105 remains the largest single-engine jet fighter yet manufactured by the United States.

On July 25, 1956, the Republic F-105 was officially named the Thunderchief by the US Air Force.[19] Earlier that summer, Republic had submitted this name to the USAF, desiring to have the F-105 carry on this firm's tradition of naming its fighter aircraft beginning with the word 'Thunder', a practice that had begun with the P-47 Thunderbolt. In July 1956, the Air Force cancelled the procurement of a reconnaissance version of the Thunderchief, the RF-105B, in favor of the McDonnell RF-101A/C Voodoo. The following year, five two-seat F-105Cs, originally ordered in June 1956, were likewise cancelled.

The F-105C had been intended for training and pilot familiarization duties. As such, it had two cockpits placed in a tandem arrangement under a large single-piece canopy. Had it been built, the F-105C would have retained an offensive capability similar to that of the single-seat aircraft, however, it

This view of an F-105B illustrates the Thunderchief's unique forward swept intakes along with its ordinance carrying capability. (USAF)

would have had a reduced fuel load and a corresponding reduction in range. Although no F-105Cs were ever produced, this variant did reach the mock-up stage prior to its cancellation.

Following the cancellation of the photoreconnaissance version of the Thunderchief, the three RF-105Bs under construction were completed as JF-105B test aircraft. As a result, space in the nose that was originally intended to house up to five separate cameras was available for the installation of test equipment. The first flight of a JF-105B took place at Farmingdale on July 18, 1957. After entering service, the three JF-105Bs saw extensive use in a variety of flight test operations in support of the Thunderchief program.

Installed inside of the F-105B's nose was a 20mm M61A1 Vulcan cannon that was fed by a drum capable of holding 1,028 rounds of 20mm ammunition. This gun also armed most single-seat versions of the Lockheed F-104 Starfighter. The F-105B's primary purpose, however, was that of a nuclear strike fighter-bomber. To fulfill that mission, the Thunderchief was designed with a large internal weapon bay measuring 15 feet 10 inches in length and 2 feet 8 inches in both width and height. Inside of the bay, a 3,400 pound nuclear weapon or a 390-gallon fuel tank could be carried.[20]

The F-105B also possessed the ability to carry up to 12,000 pounds of stores externally on five pylons, four of which could be mounted in pairs under each wing while a fifth could be installed under the fuselage on the centerline. These weapon stations provided for a wide array of loadout options that could include a combination of 500 and 750 pound bombs, 2.75-inch FFAR pods, and GAR-8 (AIM-9) Sidewinder AAMs.

Since the wing's internal volume was insufficient to allow them to carry fuel, engineers at Republic placed all of the F-105B's seven fuel tanks inside of the fuselage. Collectively, these tanks were capable of carrying 1,160 gallons of JP-4 fuel which could be augmented by the before mentioned 390 gallon auxiliary tank in the weapons bay. It was also possible for the aircraft to be fitted with up to three 450-gallon drop tanks, with two of these mounted under the wings and a single tank on the centerline station.[21]

Besides the ability to carry external fuel tanks, the F-105B also featured an extendable refueling probe on the left side of its nose. This installation was compatible with the probe and drogue method of aerial refueling then in common use with the Tactical Air Command (TAC). When the F-105 first entered service, TAC's tanker force consisted of propeller driven KB-50 and KC-97 tankers. The use of such refueling aircraft presented a serious problem for F-105 pilots as the top speed of the tanker was very near the stalling speed of their own aircraft. The fitting of auxiliary jet engines to these tankers alleviated this difficulty to some degree, although it never completely solved the problem.

It was not until the arrival of the KC-135 Stratotanker in 1957 that the Air Force possessed a truly successful tanker for the aerial refueling of jet-powered aircraft. However, since the KC-135 utilized the flying-boom method of refueling favored by the Strategic Air Command (SAC) for their bomber force, the F-105B could not receive fuel without the fitting of an adapter to the tanker's boom. Late production F-105Ds would overcome this limitation with the installation of boom compatible receptacles.

The F-105B was equipped with the General Electric MA-8 fire control system. Included in this system was a E-34 ranging radar, a E-50 gyro computing sight, and a E-30 toss-bomb computer. The aircraft was also fitted with a General Electric FC-5 flight control system and a T-145 weapons system for the delivery of nuclear weapons. In November 1957, the Air Force amended GOR 49 to specify the equipping of the Thunderchief with the AN/APN-105 Doppler navigation system.[22] During 1959, the Air Force initiated Project Optimize, which addressed deficiencies found in the F-105B's avionics and MA-8 fire control system.

The first 10 examples of the F-105B built by Republic retained the rear cockpit windows like those found in the YF-105A, however, beginning with the eleventh aircraft, these windows were deleted.[23] On May 27, 1958, the USAF accepted its first production example of the F-105B, with the 335th Tactical Fighter Squadron (TFS) of the 4th Tactical Fighter Wing (TFW) becoming operational with the type in August of that year. Due to the lengthy delays dogging the F-105 program, the 335th TFS was reassigned from their permanent station at Seymour-Johnson AFB, North Carolina to Eglin AFB, Florida in order to conduct operational testing with the Thunderchief.[24]

Two other 4th TFW units also operated the F-105B, these being the 334th and 336th Tactical Fighter Squadrons. However, the F-105B's tenure in frontline units was brief as the type began transferring to Air National Guard squadrons during 1964 following the arrival of the F-105D. On April 16, 1964, the 141st TFS of the 108th Tactical Fighter Group of the New Jersey ANG received its first F-105B.[25] The F-105B remained in Air National Guard service until its retirement in 1981, the same year that the last such aircraft was also retired from the Air Force Reserve's 466th TFS, 508th TFG, based at Hill AFB, Utah.

In May of 1963, the F-105B was selected to replace the F-100C as the mount of the USAF's aerial demonstration team, the Thunderbirds. To fulfill this role, nine F-105Bs were withdrawn from 4th TFW squadrons and flown to Republic's plant at Farmingdale to receive the modifications necessary for their new assignment. This included the removal of the M61A1 cannon, which required the addition of ballast to maintain the aircraft's center of gravity. Also removed during this process was the AN/APN-105 Doppler navigation system, and the APS-54 radar

Six F-105Bs on the flight line. The crewmen working around the second aircraft provide some idea of the Thunderchief's immense size. (USAF)

warning receiver. Two 50-gallon smoke oil tanks were installed inside of the modified aircraft's weapons bay. While all of the modified F-105Bs had their fiberglass nosecones replaced by metal ones, four of the F-105Bs involved in the modification process also received stainless steel tail fins. This change was necessary to allow the vertical stabilizers to resist the heat generated by the exhaust of other aircraft while flying in tight formation. Between January and April of 1964, Republic delivered the modified F-105Bs to the Thunderbirds at Nellis AFB, which began flying displays with the aircraft on April 26, 1964.

The Thunderbirds were flying their sixth show using the Thunderchief on May 9, 1964 when tragedy struck at Hamilton AFB, California. On that date, Captain Gene Devlin was killed when the F-105B (57-5801) he was flying broke apart during an aerial display. As a result, the Thunderbirds immediately grounded their F-105Bs. A subsequent investigation into the accident revealed that a structural splice plate in the upper fuselage had failed due to fatigue. This led to the installation of a redesigned splice plate into the entire F-105B fleet and early F-105Ds during Project Backbone.[26]

Meanwhile, the Thunderbirds decided to abandon their heavy F-105Bs, transitioning to the more maneuverable F-100D Super Sabre shortly following the crash. Since its creation in 1953, the USAF Thunderbirds have flown displays in no less than eight different aircraft types. Of these, the F-105B holds the dubious distinction of having the shortest career with the team as a display aircraft.

On December 11, 1959, the commander of the 4th TFW, Brigadier General Joseph H. Moore set a world speed record of 1,216.48 mph over a 100 km closed course at Edwards AFB in an F-105B. This shattered the previous record set in June of that year by a French Nord Griffon II experimental aircraft.

During 1957, the Air Force and Republic entered into the early planning stages for the production of an improved version of the Thunderchief, the F-105D. This model was to possess a true all-weather capability, a feature that the F-105B lacked. The manufacture of the B model ceased in December 1959 after Republic had produced just 75 examples, a number that included the 10 preproduction aircraft.

The F-105D was fitted with the more powerful Pratt & Whitney J75-P-19W turbojet. The W at the end of the engine specification signified that this engine featured a water injection system that permitted a significant increase in the thrust output of the engine. This version of the J75 was capable of generating 16,100 pounds of dry thrust and 24,500 pounds with afterburning. For short periods, water injection allowed the engine to generate 26,500 pounds of thrust, an increase of just over 8 percent of its rated thrust in afterburner. This powerplant arrangement gave the F-105D a top speed of 1,372 mph (Mach 2.08) at 36,089 feet.[27]

During its career, the F-105 received a variety of nicknames, the two most common being the "Lead Sled" and the "Thud." The former apparently originated in reference to the F-105's weight and long takeoff roll. Meanwhile, the term "Thud" has become synonymous with F-105 Thunderchief. There is no definite explanation as to how the "Thud" moniker originated, but one of the more popular beliefs is that it came into being from the sound an F-105D makes when it hits the ground.

In order to operate effectively as an all-weather fighter-bomber, the F-105D was equipped with the AN/ASG-19 Thunderstick bombing navigation system. The AN/ASG-19 included the Autonetics NASARR R-14A radar that was capable of operating in both air-to-air and air-to-ground modes. The R-14A represented a significant advancement in terms of capability compared to the E-34 ranging radar that was a component of the

MA-8 fire control system installed in the F-105B.[28]

Another change made with the D model was the replacement of several conventional circular displays in the cockpit with vertical tape style instruments. It was believed that this type of instrumentation was more easily interpreted by a pilot during operations in poor weather conditions compared to traditional dials. The AF/A42G-8 automatic flight control system was capable of operating in fully automatic modes enabling it to perform automated bomb-toss maneuvers and instrument landing approaches.[29] The avionics suite of the F-105D also included the AN/APN-131 Doppler navigation radar that was installed just behind the forward landing gear wheel well.

After being presented with a full-scale mockup of its cockpit section, the Air Force Mockup Board gave its approval to the configuration of the F-105D on December 11, 1957.[30] Externally, the F-105D was distinguishable from the earlier B model in having a longer forward fuselage and an enlarged radome. Another change made between the models was the repositioning of the pitot tube from the port wing to the radome of the F-105D. Not counting the pitot tube, the F-105D had a length of 64 feet 5 inches, making it 1 foot 4 inches longer than the F-105B. Nonetheless, both the B and the D models were identical in wingspan and height.

During 1958, Republic argued that although the F-105D was generally similar to the B model, the differences between the two models were sufficient to make it difficult to use the same production line that had fabricated the F-105B. To cope with the increasing weight of the Thunderchief, a stronger landing gear and new brakes had to be developed. The inlet ducts also required modifications to accommodate the requirements of the upgraded engine. Issues such as these led Republic to increase the production lead-time for each aircraft from 144 to 214 workdays.[31]

In 1958, Republic began the development of a two-seat trainer variant of the D model, designated as the F-105E. The design of this aircraft drew heavily upon the experience gained during the development of the cancelled F-105C, including the placement of the pilots in tandem cockpits under a single-piece canopy. For presentation to the Air Force, Republic took the mockup it had built to represent the F-105C and fitted it with instrumentation from the F-105D. Initially, the Air Force favored the acquisition of the F-105E and placed an order for 26 examples in late 1958.[32] On March 18, 1959, however, the Air Force cancelled the acquisition of the F-105E to free up funds for the F-105D. Had the two-seat F-105E been produced, it would have had the same overall dimensions as the D model.

In common with the F-105B, the F-105D was equipped with the M61A1 Vulcan cannon, although with the cost and weight of the aircraft growing at an alarming rate some consideration was later given towards the deletion of this weapon. This was one of the recommendations made by a committee of USAF officers formed to review what features could be removed from the F-105D to cut costs without impairing its ability to perform its primary mission. Since, the Thunderchief's intended role was to conduct strike operations using either nuclear or conventional weapons, several members of the committee felt that the gun served little purpose on an operational level. This perception was strongly disapproved of by some of the other board members that held an opposing viewpoint on the value of maintaining the M61A1. In the final analysis, however, the cannon was retained, a fortuitous decision that was validated just a few years later during the F-105's involvement in the air war over Southeast Asia (SEA).

The F-105D's ability to carry a maximum 14,000 pounds of ordinance represented a nearly 17 percent increase over the F-105B's 12,000 pound warload. Both aircraft shared the same number of pylons, one on the centerline and four on the wings. With a MK-28 special stores payload, the F-105D had a combat radius of 625 miles, which could be increased to 778 miles if its external drop tanks were not dropped before entering combat. Loaded with 3,100 gallons of fuel this aircraft had a ferry range of 2,206 miles at an average speed of 583 mph.[33]

On June 9, 1959, Republic test pilot Lindell Hendrix took the first F-105D (58-1146) on its maiden flight at Farmingdale. Despite the Thunderchief program enduring a number of delays and production slippages, the first flight of the F-105D actually occurred one month earlier than scheduled. As were its predecessors, the YF-105A and F-105B, the F-105D was reported to be a very stable and well handling aircraft.

On September 28, 1960, the F-105D was formally accepted by the Tactical Air Command, although the type would not be declared operational until the following year. As had taken place during the service entry of the F-105B, the 4th TFW's 335th TFS became the first USAF unit to receive the new model of the Thunderchief. Furthermore, since the 335th TFS would conduct

Shown here at Republic Aviation's plant at Farmingdale, New York is the first F-105D built (58-1146). (USAF)

Category II flight-testing of the D model, it was once again temporarily reassigned to Eglin AFB. By the time that the F-105D entered operational service in 1961, three other units of the 4th TFW had also received the type, these being the 333th, 334th, and 336th Tactical Fighter Squadrons. Unlike the F-105B, which served only with the 4th TFW while it was in frontline service, the F-105D was more widely deployed once becoming operational. This included its posting to Pacific Air Forces (PACAF) units. The first such unit to receive the F-105D was the 18th TFW at Kadena AB, Okinawa in October 1962, which was followed by the 8th TFW based at Itazuke AB, Japan when it began operating the Thunderchief early the following year.

The early 1960s witnessed an escalation in the Cold War between East and West. As the USAF's premier strike fighter-bomber, the F-105D was a natural choice for deployment to the Federal Republic of Germany. In May 1961, the F-105D entered service with the 36th TFW at Bitburg AB, this being followed later by the type's arrival at Spangdahlem where it joined the 49th TFW. Had war broken out in Europe, these F-105s would have been tasked with deep strike missions into Eastern Europe. The superb performance capabilities of the F-105D combined with its ability to deliver a sizable payload accurately onto a target in nearly any weather condition made this aircraft a major threat to the Warsaw Pact.

In December 1961, the USAF issued a grounding order affecting all of their F-105Ds when the main fuselage frame of a test article failed during fatigue testing at Wright-Patterson AFB, Ohio. A further analysis revealed that despite suffering a fracture, the frame retained a great deal of its original strength. This problem was quickly resolved when Republic provided the necessary tools and adapters to carry out the necessary corrective actions.[34]

In June of 1962, the USAF grounded all of its F-105B and D

An F-105D (59-1719) in flight. This photograph provides another view of the Thunderchief's unique shaped air intakes for its J75 engine. (USAF)

Thunderchiefs following two accidents at Nellis AFB. This resulted in a modification program to correct wire chafing and flight control issues designated as Project Look Alike. This process brought all of the earlier F-105Ds up to the F-105D-25RE standard. Look Alike modifications also quadrupled the F-105D's previous capability of carrying just four 750 pound bombs to sixteen mounted on multiple ejector racks. Early F-105 operations had revealed that the aircraft's natural metal finish was susceptible to corrosion, leading to moisture entering the equipment bays. The solution devised to correct this problem was to spray the Thunderchief with aluminized lacquer that sealed the seams, thereby preventing further issues caused by water seepage.[35]

As with many other facets of the F-105 program, Look Alike proved to take longer and cost significantly more than originally forecasted. In 1962, at the beginning of the project, it was estimated that the modification program could be quickly accomplished. However, the last aircraft to receive Look Alike modifications was not completed until mid-1964, some two years and 51 million dollars later. Despite various fixes, the F-105D fleet continued to suffer a number of accidents due to engine failures, and fuel system malfunctions during this timeframe.[36] In fact, between 1960 and 1965 no less than sixty F-105Ds were lost, resulting in the type being grounded on numerous occasions.[37]

The final F-105D was delivered by Republic to the Air Force in January 1964 after 610 examples had been built, making it the definitive Thunderchief model. This number was considerably less than the USAF's original procurement plan that envisioned 1,500 F-105Ds equipping 14 wings. This reduction resulted from a decision made by Secretary of Defense Robert S. McNamara to slash the size of the Thunderchief's acquisition due to budgetary considerations.

On August 7, 1964, the US Congress adopted the Gulf of Tonkin Resolution following a series of engagements between North Vietnamese gunboats and US Navy warships. This event signaled the beginning of an increased involvement by the

An F-105D (62-4234) with a full load of bombs. During the early days of its involvement in the air war over Southeast Asia, F-105s retained their bare metal finishes. (USAF)

United States in the Vietnam War. The first F-105s to arrive in SEA belonged to the 36th TFS following their deployment from Yokota AB, Japan to Korat RTAB, Thailand on August 9, 1964. Initially, these aircraft operated over Laos on missions supporting CIA operations.

The rapidly increasing tempo of US military operations in SEA led to the deployment of additional F-105 squadrons, including the 44th, 67th, 80th, and 357th Tactical Fighter Squadrons.[38] The first loss of a Thunderchief to enemy fire occurred shortly after the type arrived in theater. On August 14, 1964, a 36th TFS F-105D piloted by Lieutenant Dave Graben was struck by ground fire during a Rescue Combat Air Patrol (RESCAP) mission over Laos. Although heavily damaged, the Thunderchief's inherit ruggedness allowed Graben to fly back to Korat where he made a safe landing. Graben's F-105D, however, was so significantly damaged that it was later written off as a total loss.

Beginning on December 14, 1964, F-105s were tasked to provide air support to Royal Laotian troops under the auspices of Operation Barrel Roll. Five days later, the Thunderchief was involved in its first Barrel Roll strike when F-105s belonging to the 80th TFS attacked two bridges near the village of Nape in central Laos. In what would come to characterize the air war in SEA, the strike was governed by strict rules of engagement. The first step of the mission involved the F-105s flying from their base at Takhli, Thailand to Da Nang, South Vietnam where they were armed and refueled. This was influenced by the 1962 Geneva Accords, which stipulated that only aircraft based in South Vietnam were permitted to attack targets in Laos. Furthermore, the strike package, which also included RF-101C Voodoos and F-100D Super Sabres, was forced to fly into northern Laos before heading south towards its target. Additional restrictions were also imposed upon the actual strike itself, serving to further complicate the mission.

Following a Viet Cong attack against a US camp at Pleiku on February 7, 1965, Operation Flaming Dart began with the first F-105 air strikes against targets in North Vietnam. This was followed by Flaming Dart II, which saw a continuation of attacks against the North. Such operations had the effect of bringing additional F-105s into SEA. The air war over Vietnam greatly intensified with the beginning of Operation Rolling Thunder on March 2, 1965. Rolling Thunder called for a sustained aerial bombardment campaign against the North by units of the USAF, the US Navy, and the Republic of Vietnam's Air Force (VNAF).

On the first day of Rolling Thunder, three F-105Ds belonging to the 67th TFS were lost during attack missions against targets in North Vietnam. Such losses were a portent of things to come, as the Thunderchief would go on to conduct the majority of the airstrikes against the North during the campaign. As the requirement for fighter-bombers increased in SEA during Rolling Thunder, the PACAF began regular rotations of F-105 squadrons through both Korat and Takhli RTABs.[39] By the spring of 1966, the PACAF had established two permanent F-105 wings in Thailand. The first of these was the 355th TFW when it was established at Takhli on November 8, 1965, this being followed on April 8, 1966 by the activation of the 388th TFW at Korat.

As had been witnessed during earlier bombing operations conducted in SEA, Operation Rolling Thunder was heavily influenced by political considerations. This resulted in the creation of stringent rules of engagement for US airmen, which were strictly enforced. Furthermore, the selection of targets was subject to a complex path up the chain of command, which ended with President Lyndon B. Johnson's final approval, or rejection. Such political micromanagement severely limited the effectiveness of the campaign and resulted in a further increase of the danger facing US aircrews over the North. During 1965,

Three F-105Ds refuel from a KC-135 Stratotanker. The three fighter-bombers in the foreground have received camouflage paint schemes while a fourth in the background retains a silver finish. (USAF)

President Johnson ordered two separate bombing halts in an attempt to entice North Vietnam to begin peace negotiations. However, these gestures accomplished little more than providing the North an opportunity to replenish and strengthen its air defenses.

While deployed to SEA, the F-105D received a number of modifications resulting from experiences gained during combat operations. During 1965, the F-105 fleet began receiving a camouflage paint scheme. As much of Vietnam is heavily forested, such a color pattern helped minimize the chances that F-105s operating at low level would be sighted by highflying enemy fighters. Combat operations had also demonstrated that the F-105's primary and secondary hydraulic systems were located too close together, thereby maximizing the chances of both systems being affected by the same battle damage. To reduce this vulnerability, a third hydraulic system was later installed in the Thunderchief. The growing threat posed by

165

radar directed SAM sites in the North also led to the installation of Radar Homing and Warning (RHAW) antennas to the lower nose section and on top of the tail.

Operation Rolling Thunder concluded on November 1, 1968. During the entire campaign, the F-105D had remained the USAF's primary fighter-bomber in SEA. In October of that same year, the Korat based 388th TFW began transitioning to the F-4E Phantom II, their F-105s being transferred to the 355th TFW at Takhli, which became the sole Thunderchief unit remaining in SEA.[40] The final F-105D bombing mission of the Vietnam War was flown on October 9, 1970. When the last F-105D departed Takhli in December of that year, the only remaining Thunderchiefs in SEA were 12 F-105G Wild Weasels assigned to the 6010th Wild Weasel Squadron. Between July 1965 and November 1972, the F-105 conducted more than 20,000 missions over Vietnam.

The increasing effectiveness of the North's air defense system during the war combined with the hazardous nature of the missions performed by the Thunderchief led to the type suffering horrendous losses during the Vietnam War. During a period beginning in 1965 and ending in 1972, no less than 321 F-105s of all types were lost to enemy fire, while a further 61 aircraft were destroyed in operational accidents. The combined total of these losses represents 46% of the total 833 F-105s built. This loss rate would have been significantly higher had it not been for the inherit strength of the Thunderchief's design. On numerous occasions, F-105s were able to return to base after sustaining damage that most other aircraft could not have survived. In one example, an F-105D (60-5376) was able to recover after being struck by a US AIM-9 Sidewinder missile.[41] During the F-105's involvement in SEA, 130 pilots and Electronic Warfare Officers (EWOs) were listed as being either Killed in Action (KIA) or Missing in Action (MIA), while an additional 90 Thunderchief crewmen were captured.

During the Vietnam War, 17 F-105s were lost in aerial combat to North Vietnamese MiG-17 and MiG-21 fighters. The heavy Thunderchief, however, managed to score 27 ½ victories against the more nimble MiG-17. With three exceptions, all of these kills were made with the F-105's M61A1 Vulcan cannon.[42] The first F-105 air combat victory took place on June 29, 1966 when a F-105D belonging to the 388th TFW and flown by Major Fred L. Tracy shot down a MiG-17. On May 13, 1967, one of the highest scoring days for US fighter pilots during the Vietnam War occurred, during which five separate F-105Ds shot down an equal number of MiG-17s. The final F-105 aerial victories of the war were scored on December 19, 1967, when two F-105Fs from 355th TFW each managed to down a MiG-17, with one of the Thunderchiefs sharing credit for its kill with a 8th TFW F-4D Phantom II.[43]

In 1969, the USAF approved Fairchild Republic's proposal to upgrade the AN/ASG-19 Thunderstick bombing system to improve its accuracy and blind bombing ability.[44] Designated as Thunderstick II, this enhancement incorporated a modified Singer-General Precision inertial reference unit and gyrocompass. The modification process also included the replacement of the Sperry AN/ARN-85 LORAN receiver, which had proven difficult and expensive to maintain.[45] In its place, an International Telephone & Telegraph (ITT) AN/ARN-92 digital receiver was installed. Improvements were also made to the AN/APN-131 Doppler navigation radar while the Autonetics R-14 radar was upgraded to the R-14K standard with solid-state circuitry which resulted in improved radar returns.

Fairchild Republic upgraded thirty F-105Ds with Thunderstick II modifications between early 1969 and July 1971. These aircraft were easily identifiable by a fairing that extended along top of the fuselage from the rear of the cockpit to the vertical stabilizer. Flight tests of the system began at Eglin AFB in September 1969 and progressed rapidly before being completed in November of that year. Although Thunderstick II provided an improvement in the F-105D's bombing capabilities, the system required a high level of maintenance on an operational level. On top of this, only when everything was in perfect working order could a Circular Error Probability (CEP) of less than 500 feet be met.[46]

Following modifications, F-105Ds upgraded with Thunderstick II equipment were assigned to the 563rd TFS of the 23rd TFW at McConnell AFB, Kansas. In 1972, the USAF transferred these aircraft to the 457th TFS of the 301st TFW, a unit belonging to the Air Force Reserve based at Carswell AFB, Texas. The 457th TFS continued operating the F-105D until retiring the type near the end of 1982.[47]

The lack of a two-place variant of the Thunderchief led to the

A Republic F-105D (60-0521) upgraded to Thunderstick II standards, which can be determined by the fairing between the cockpit and vertical stabilizer. Also illustrated are the petal sections of the F-105's exhaust nozzle. (USAF)

consideration of utilizing the F-100F Super Sabre as a proficiency and transitional trainer for prospective F-105 pilots.[48] However, given the relative scarcity of the F-100F, its use as an F-105 training platform was somewhat impractical. In an effort to alleviate this issue, the Tactical Air Command outfitted six T-39B Sabreliner utility training aircraft with NASARR and Doppler radar equipment to train pilots on the F-105's navigation and bombing systems.[49]

In May of 1962, Secretary of Defense McNamara authorized the acquisition of a dual place version of the Thunderchief designated as the F-105F. The Air Force ordered the conversion of the last 143 F-105Ds on order into an equivalent number of F-105Fs. Republic received $8 million to cover the costs associated with the revised contract. As no further aircraft were procured, all F-105Fs built had been originally ordered as F-105Ds.

The F-105F differed from Republic's previous dual-place Thunderchief proposals, the F-105C and E, in placing the aft crewmember under a separate canopy rather than having both cockpits sharing a large single-piece canopy. To accommodate the second cockpit, the fuselage of the F-105F was thirty-one inches longer than the D model. The aircraft also featured a vertical fin that was increased in both height and chord. Both cockpits were equipped with dual flight controls, with the student pilot occupying the forward cockpit. The F-105F was fitted with an avionics suite identical to that installed in the F-105D.

The F-105F retained the M61A1 Vulcan cannon of the F-105D along with the capability of carrying a weapons payload equal to 14,000 pounds. The F model was also equipped with the same Pratt & Whitney J75-P-19W turbojet that powered the D model. The lengthened fuselage allowed both models to possess an identical internal fuel load of 1,026 gallons. With a gross weight of 54,580 pounds, however, the F-105F was nearly 2,000 pounds

Unlike two previous proposals that had incorporated a single piece canopy, the two-seat F-105F featured separate canopies for each cockpit. (USAF)

heavier than the F-105D, thereby requiring strengthened main landing gear struts.[50] Since the F-105F shared such a high degree of commonality with the F-105D, it did not require an extensive flight test program. However, this same characteristic also meant that the F-105F suffered from the same problems found in the F-105D, thus requiring both models to receive similar refits.

The F-105F prototype was rolled out of Republic's factory at Farmingdale on May 23, 1963, some 40 days ahead of schedule. The first flight took place a few weeks later on June 11, 1963, during which the aircraft (62-4412) reached a speed of Mach 1.15. The F-105F entered operational service with the 4th TFW at Seymour-Johnson AFB on December 23, 1963. In January 1965, the final F-105F was delivered to the Air Force, marking the end of Thunderchief production after some 833 F-105s of various models had been produced.

After entering operational service, it was typical to have a small number of F-105Fs assigned to each F-105D squadron for transitional and proficiency purposes. When Thunderchief squadrons began deploying to SEA during 1964, the F-105F accompanied the single-seat models into the war zone. Possessing a full combat capability, many F-105Fs were assigned bombing missions as the conflict intensified. The increasing lethality of North Vietnam's air defenses prompted the Air Force to improve its ability to counter such systems. This led to the development of tactics and equipment for aircraft that were specially configured to hinder an enemy's air defense capability. During the Vietnam War, such aircraft were known as Wild Weasels, a term originating from the project's name that had led to their development. Today, these types of operations are termed as the Suppression of Enemy Air Defenses (SEAD) role.

Possessing a substantial payload capacity along with a second cockpit in which an additional crewmember could be placed to handle a variety of new electronic devices, the F-105F was a logical choice as a Wild Weasel platform. At the time, the F-105D was the USAF's primary strike fighter-bomber in SEA, thus the F-105F's nearly identical performance capabilities further enhanced the type's suitability as an escorting Wild Weasel aircraft.

In January 1966, Fairchild Republic began modifying the first of an eventual eighty-six F-105Fs to the Wild Weasel III standard. Aircraft that had undergone this conversion process were equipped with AN/APR-25/26 RHAW receivers, an IR-133 panoramic scan receiver, a KA-60 panoramic camera, and a combat event tape recorder. After receiving Wild Weasel III modifications, these aircraft were unofficially designated as EF-105Fs, although they retained their official F-105F designation. By the summer of 1966, thirteen refitted F-105Fs were deployed to SEA, which were followed by the arrival of ten additional examples over the next three months. The final F-105F converted to the Wild Weasel III specification was completed in March 1968.[51]

In Wild Weasel F-105s, the rear seat was occupied by an Electronic Warfare Office (EWO). The EWO, or Bear as he became known, operated the various pieces of electronic equipment installed onboard the aircraft designed to detect and determine the position of enemy radars. In such an arrangement, the pilot remained the aircraft's commander and was responsible for its operation and safety. In combat situations, however, the Bear's role became critical as he had the most complete picture of the danger posed by the enemy's air defense network and was therefore in a position to provide the pilot with instructions to meet that threat. As one Thunderchief pilot put it, "Nobody will actually second guess a Bear. You might do so in peacetime, but you don't do it in war."

In addition to the electronic equipment installed during their upgrade to Wild Weasels, converted F-105Fs were also given the capability to fire the AGM-45A Shrike Anti-Radiation Missile (ARM). Developed at China Lake, California by the Naval Weapons Center during the early 1960s the Shrike first entered

An F-105F (63-8280) and an F-105D (62-4355) fly in formation over Japan, near Mt. Fuji. (USAF)

service with US Navy attack squadrons during 1964. The AGM-45A had a maximum range of 10 miles and became operational with the USAF in SEA during 1966 following its adoption as a standard penetration aid.[52] The AGM-45A had two distinct limitations, however, the first being that it could only home in on a radar as long as it continued transmitting. If, however, the targeted radar shut down, the Shrike would lose its lock and follow an unguided path to the ground. Secondly, the AGM-45A had an effective range that was less than half that of its chief adversary, the SA-2 SAM system, thereby requiring the launching aircraft to come within lethal range of its target. Despite its faults, the Shrike provided the F-105F with an effective method to either destroy an enemy radar emitter or at least force it to shut down, either of which constituted a successful Wild Weasel mission.

In a project that concluded during February 1968, 14 F-105Fs received modifications permitting them to fire the new longer-ranged AGM-78A Standard Anti-Radiation Missile. Built by the General Dynamics Corporation, the Standard ARM initially incorporated the same seeker head found in the AGM-45 Shrike. By 1969, however, an upgraded version, the AGM-78B, equipped with a memory chip that recorded the coordinates of a radar emitter became available. This enabled the missile to home in on an emitter's location even if it ceased transmitting. In November 1968, a program to equip 16 F-105Fs with the capability to fire the AGM-78B began, which continued through June of the following year.[53]

Fighter pilots belonging to the North Vietnamese Air Force received Soviet style training that emphasized the rigid ground control of air interceptions, leaving little room for individual initiative. To exploit this weakness, at least a dozen F-105Fs were equipped with Hallicrafters QRC-128 VHF jammers to block communication links between North Vietnamese fighter pilots and their ground controllers. This modification took place during 1967 under a project code named Combat Martin. As the QRC-128 was a large piece of equipment, its installation required the removal of the ejection seat from the rear cockpit. Pilots of Combat Martin F-105Fs often used the moniker "Colonel Computer" to describe their new backseater. All F-105Fs equipped with QRC-128 jamming equipment were identifiable by a large aerial fitted on the top of the fuselage just behind the rear canopy. Following the deactivation of the 355th TFW in December 1970, surviving Combat Martin F-105Fs were modified to F-105G Wild Weasel specifications.[54]

On October 31, 1968, President Lyndon B. Johnson ordered a halt to all bombing missions against North Vietnam in another effort to entice the North Vietnamese government to begin peace talks. However, reconnaissance flights over the North were allowed to continue. To perform these missions, the USAF utilized the RF-4C Phantom II, and supported by F-105 Wild Weasels.

On February 23, 1970, the USAF authorized the modification

A Republic F-105G in flight carrying a pair of AGM-45 Shrikes on the outboard pylons, and a AGM-78 Standard ARM on the left inboard station. (USAF)

of 54 F-105Fs into an enhanced Wild Weasel variant designated as the F-105G. A significant component of this conversion was the elimination of the need to carry an ECM pod, either a Hughes ALQ-71 or a General Electric ALQ-87, on one of the outboard wing pylons. The carrying of such pods, mandated by the US Seventh Air Force during 1967, meant that one less weapon station was available on each individual sortie. Recognizing this deficiency, the Air Force teamed up with Fairchild Republic and Westinghouse to formulate a possible solution. Their answer was to split a Westinghouse AN/ALQ-101 ECM pod in half, and attach both halves to each side of the F-105's lower fuselage just below the wings. Later, the modified jamming pod received the AN/ALQ-105 designation.[55]

The F-105G conversion also included the installation of the Itek AN/APR-35/36/37 RHAW systems which replaced the aircraft's existing AN/APR-25/26 RHAW equipment produced by the same manufacturer. Other electronic equipment installed into the F-105G included a Bendix APS-107 target acquisition set and a Loral AN/ALR-31 RHAW receiver. The latter system involved the installation of antennas on the wingtips, thus requiring the repositioning of the navigational lights from their original locations to mounts on the leading edges of the wings.

Although, cleared to carry a wide variety of ordinance, the F-105G's standard armament loadout for operational missions normally consisted of a pair of AGM-45 Shrikes on the outboard pylons, one AGM-78 Standard on the left inboard pylon, one 450 gallon drop tank on the right inboard station, and a 650 gallon tank on the centerline pylon. This was in addition to the standard M61A1 Vulcan cannon in the nose with 1,028 round of ammunition.

Conversions of the F-105F to the F-105G specification were performed by Fairchild Republic at Farmingdale, and by the USAF at the McClellan AFB, California. Deliveries of the F-105G to the Tactical Air Command began on June 9, 1970.[56] To assist in the training of F-105G EWOs, the Air Force outfitted three T-39A Sabreliners with Wild Weasel electronic equipment and antennas. Following their conversion, these aircraft were redesignated as T-39Fs.

When the 355th TFW stood down at Takhli RTAB, Thailand in December 1970, all of its F-105s with the exception of 12 F-105Gs were transferred to McConnell AFB, Kansas. The remaining F-105Gs flew to Korat RTAB where they joined the newly formed 6010th Wild Weasel Squadron (WWS).[57] After replacing Detachment One, 12th TFS, the 6010th WWS became the last remaining unit operating the F-105 Thunderchief in SEA. The 6010th WWS was later redesignated as the 17th WWS on December 1, 1971.

The F-105G continued to serve in SEA throughout the balance of America's involvement in the Vietnam War. When Operation Linebacker began on May 10, 1972, only 16 F-105Gs belonging to the 17th WWS remained in SEA.[58] These aircraft were later reinforced by an additional 12 F-105Gs deployed from McConnell AFB. Operation Linebacker was the first aerial offensive carried out against the North since the 1968 bombing halt, and continued until October 23, 1972, during which time no less than 4 F-105Gs had been lost to hostile fire. Following a brief pause, the bombing of the North resumed on December 18, 1972, with the beginning of Operation Linebacker II. Although this aerial bombardment campaign only lasted eleven days, it witnessed the heaviest bombing raids of the entire Vietnam War. As before, the F-105G was once again tasked with protecting strike packages from the North's air defenses. The Thunderchief's lengthy operational career in SEA ended on October 29, 1974 when the final F-105G departed Thailand.

Upon their return stateside, all of the 17th WWS's F-105Gs were transferred to the 562nd TFS at George AFB, California,

An F-105G belonging to the 128th TFS, 116th TFW, of the Georgia Air National Guard thunders into the air during the twilight of its career. (DI)

where they joined the 35th TFW's other F-105G squadron, the 561st TFS. The F-105G remained in active service with the USAF until being fully replaced in frontline units by the F-4G Phantom II. Following this, surviving G models were reassigned to the 128th TFS, 116th TFW, of the Georgia Air National Guard. The 128th TFS operated the F-105G until retiring the type in 1983.

The F-105 Thunderchief and Convair's F-106 Delta Dart were the only two Century Series fighters not exported to foreign users. In July 1960, however, Republic offered the F-105D to Britain's Royal Air Force and France's Armée de l'Air. The offer made to the Royal Air Force included an option for the installation of the Bristol Olympus B.01.22R turbojet that had been developed for the BAC TSR-2. In the end, neither Britain nor France proceeded forward with either of Republic's proposals.[59]

Following their retirement, most F-105s arrived at the Military Aircraft Storage and Disposition Center (MASDC) at Davis-Monthan AFB, Arizona.[60] Along with the F-101 Voodoo, the F-105 Thunderchief was one of two Century Series fighters not converted into a drone. Consequently, following their arrival at MASDC, many retired F-105s were scrapped within a relatively short period of time. Prior to disposal, some F-105s were used for battle damage repair training and ballistic testing. Although none of their type is airworthy today, a large number of Thunderchiefs are preserved as museum aircraft. At least ninety F-105s are on display in various locations around the United States, while a small number of additional Thunderchiefs have been likewise preserved in other nations around the globe.

# Chapter Six
## Convair F-106 Delta Dart

During the twentieth century, the industrial might of the United States was untouched by two global conflicts. Following the end of the Second World War, this nation, and a former ally, the Soviet Union, became bitter political and military rivals. Previously protected by vast oceans to the east and west, the development of long-range bombers threatened to upset the defensibility of the United States from direct enemy attack. The perceived threat posed by the Soviet Union became paramount with the communist state's detonation of its first atomic bomb in 1949. After enjoying a nuclear monopoly that had lasted only four years, the United States was suddenly confronted by an opposing power that also possessed the most destructive weapon ever created.

The development of nuclear weapons caused a significant shift in the effectiveness of strategic aerial bombing. During the Second World War, all of the primary belligerents conducted bombing campaigns of some level against their enemies. The unparalleled production capability of the United States allowed it to conduct two major bombing campaigns during the war, one against Japan, and another against Germany in cooperation with Britain. The bombardment of Japan culminated with the atomic bombings of Hiroshima and Nagasaki during August 1945. Such multi-year campaigns had involved thousands of individual sorties, representing a major investment in a nation's resources and manpower. However, the nuclear bomb changed all of this, as it was now possible to destroy an entire city with just a single bomb. Realizing that by the early 1950s, the Soviet Union would be able to marry nuclear weapons to its bomber force, US military planners realized that, for the first time, American cities would be vulnerable to annihilation by enemy bomber attack.

Protecting the Continental United States against such an airborne attack was the responsibility of the USAF's Air Defense Command (ADC). Between 1950 and 1953, the ADC placed three new jet interceptors into service, these being the Northrop F-89 Scorpion, the Lockheed F-94 Starfire, and the North American F-86D Sabre. Both the F-86D and the F-94 were interceptor versions of successful first generation jet aircraft designs, these being the F-86 Sabre and the T-33 Shooting Star respectively. The F-89 Scorpion, however, was an all-new aircraft developed in response to a 1945 US Army Air Forces requirement for a jet-powered night fighter.[1]

All three of these aircraft had limitations that complicated ADC's arduous task of defending the vast expanses of North America from enemy aircraft. The fastest of these interceptors was the F-86D Sabre, which thanks to its afterburning General Electric J47 turbojet engine had a top speed of just over 700 mph, despite being nearly 50-percent heavier than its older brother, the F-86A. Although later versions of the F-89 would be capable of employing guided air-to-air missiles, the principal armament of the ADC's interceptor force during the early years of the 1950s was the 2.75-inch "Mighty Mouse" FFAR (Folding Fin Aerial Rocket). These unguided rockets were wildly inaccurate and were fired in salvoes utilizing fire-control radar systems installed in the launching aircraft to maximize their chances of downing an aerial target. Despite the F-86D, F-89, and F-94 offering performances and capabilities unheard of only a decade earlier, they were still inadequate to provide a truly effective shield against a major enemy attack.

To counter the threat posed by Soviet bombers, what the Air Defense Command really required was an interceptor force composed of long-range supersonic all-weather fighter aircraft. Due to the nature of their mission, it was also necessary for such aircraft to possess a superior rate of climb, a high ceiling, and the capability of employing guided air-to-air missiles. To achieve this, the Air Force embarked upon the 1954 Interceptor Program during 1949, which resulted in the USAF's first operational delta-wing jet fighter, the Convair F-102.

As the F-102A Delta Dagger began entering service with the Air Defense Command during the spring of 1956, the first YF-102B, a significantly improved model, was undergoing assembly at Convair's San Diego, California plant. As related in Chapter 3, the YF-102B was the result of the Air Force's earlier decision to acquire the F-102A as an "Interim Interceptor" following significant delays being encountered during the development of the Hughes MX-1179 (later MA-1) fire control system and the Wright J67 engine. At the time, the Air Force intended to procure the F-102B as an enhanced version of the Delta Dagger, once solutions for problems concerning the fire control system and engine had been established.

The developmental history of the F-102 was so troubled that if it had not been for the threat posed by the Soviet Union, there is a strong likelihood that the Air Force would have cancelled the program. In fact, the reallocation of funds to correct issues encountered by the F-102A caused the F-102B to slip behind schedule. In early 1955, recognizing that continuing difficulties with the development of the Wright J67 turbojet were to cause even further delays in acquiring the F-102B, the Air Force decided to proceed forward by substituting the Pratt & Whitney J75 engine. The J75 was the same powerplant used by the Republic F-105 Thunderchief, and was itself an improved version

This view of the first YF-106A (56-0451) illustrates its similarity to the F-102A Delta Dagger. The Delta Dart was the last dedicated interceptor built for the US Air Force. (USAF)

of the J57 engine that powered the F-102A Delta Dagger.

In November 1955, the Air Force placed an initial procurement order with Convair for 17 F-102B test aircraft, which was finalized on April 18, 1956.[2] Although the Dagger served as the basis for the F-102B, the incorporation of a large number of design revisions created what amounted to a virtually new aircraft that possessed little similarity with its predecessor. This prompted the USAF to change its designation to the F-106 on June 17, 1956.[3] During mid-1957, the F-106 was officially named the Delta Dart.

While appearing generally similar to its predecessor, the F-102A, the F-106 sported a longer fuselage, a squared off vertical fin, and redesigned air intakes that were positioned higher and further back on the fuselage. The F-106's fuselage also exhibited a much more pronounced pinching between the wing's forward and trailing edges than was found in the Dagger. Additionally, since the area rule theory had been better incorporated into its design, the F-106 did not require the tail mounted aerodynamic fairings found in the F-102A. From an aerodynamic standpoint, these differences represented a considerable improvement over the F-102A, which had received its area rule modifications during the later part of its development as an effort to overcome transonic drag problems inherit to its original design. The F-106 also sported a twin nosewheel configuration, in contrast to the Dagger's single nosewheel.

Following its completion at San Diego in November 1956, the first of two YF-106As was transported to Edwards AFB to begin the flight test phase of the program. On Wednesday, December 26, 1956, Convair test pilot Richard "Dick" L. Johnson, the same individual whom had piloted the YF-102 on its first flight, took the YF-106A aloft for the first time. Early the following year, on February 26, 1957, the second YF-106A also began flight operations at Edwards. Early test flights were conducted by Convair test pilots, these being followed by the first flight of an F-106 by a USAF pilot on April 29, 1957.[4]

Early test flights indicated that the F-106A's maximum speed and acceleration capabilities fell below expectations, despite the aircraft demonstrating its ability to reach Mach 1.9 and an altitude of 57,000 feet. During testing, it was determined that the F-106A required 4 ½ minutes to accelerate from Mach 1.0 to Mach 1.7, and an additional 2 ½ minutes to reach Mach 1.8.[5] In an effort to correct the poor acceleration issue, the USAF approved a September 1957 proposal from Convair to increase the capture area of the aircraft's ducts and a thinning of the duct lips to improve airflow to the J75-P-9 engine. The J75-P-9 engine also suffered from reliability difficulties that were addressed with the subsequent installation of the more powerful J75-P-17 turbojet.

In early 1957, the high costs associated with the F-106 coinciding with a shortage of funds for Air Force projects forced a reappraisal of the program, thus placing it into jeopardy of being cancelled.[6] The number of lengthy delays experienced during the development of the F-106, which stretched all the way back to the difficulties experienced with the F-102, had forced the Air Defense Command to find alternatives to field a viable force of interceptors.  This included the acquisition of the F-101B Voodoo interceptor, as well as building the F-102A Delta Dagger, in larger numbers than had been originally anticipated. Intended to be an interim type, pending the arrival of the F-102B (F-106), the production run of the F-102A reached 1,000 aircraft. Even by the standards of the 1950s, this figure could hardly be considered representative of a temporary measure in the procurement of increasingly expensive jet fighter aircraft.

Faced with financial difficulties, the Air Force considered dropping the F-101B interceptor in order to procure the F-106. The Air Defense Command, however, argued that to provide an

Three Air Defense Command F-106As in formation.  The Delta Dart's lengthy active-duty career spanned nearly thirty years. (USAF)

effective level of protection against enemy bombers it was necessary to acquire both the F-101B and the F-106A. In the end, the ADC successfully retained both programs, but consequently, the actual procurement of the F-106 Delta Dart was to be much smaller than originally envisioned. It was also during this time that the threat against North America began to shift away from the Soviet Union's bomber force to that nation's growing Intercontinental Ballistic Missile (ICBM) capability.

Measuring 70 feet 9 inches in length, the F-106 had a wingspan of 38 feet 4 inches, and a height of 20 feet 4 inches. These dimensions made it slightly larger, but generally similar in size to the F-102A Delta Dagger. With a maximum gross weight of 38,729 pounds, however, the F-106A weighed nearly twenty-four percent more than the F-102A.[7] Despite being heavier, the F-106A had a top speed of 1,525 mph, which made it nearly twice as fast as the F-102A. This was primarily due to its Pratt & Whitney J75-P-17 engine that was capable of producing 24,500 pounds of thrust in afterburner. Early F-106s were fitted with boundary layer fences on their wings similar to those found on the Delta Dagger, which were replaced early in the program by slots that reduced both drag and weight.

The cockpit layout of the F-106 was dominated by the radarscope that was mounted at the top center of the instrument panel. At the bottom of this panel, and between the pilot's knees, was the Tactical Situation Display (TSD). This was a circular screen upon which symbols representing the F-106 and its target were displayed in their relative positions over a moving map display. Early F-106s were equipped with conventional instrument displays, while later models were fitted with the Integrated Flight Instrument System that incorporated vertical tape style instrumentation. To eliminate glare issues stemming from the flat glass panels of the F-106's windscreen, a solid black panel called a vision splitter was installed in the center of the windscreen in the same manner as had been done in the F-102A to cure an identical problem.

In common with the Delta Dagger, the F-106's sole purpose was to operate as a missile-armed interceptor. To this end, the installation of a gun was not deemed necessary, an omission that would be rectified to some degree later in its career. The F-106 carried all of its air-to-air weaponry inside of an internal weapons bay located on the underside of the fuselage that was equipped with pneumatically operated double folding doors.

The missile armament of the F-106 consisted of 4 Hughes AIM-4 Falcon missiles and 1 AIR-2A Genie nuclear-armed unguided rocket. Although the missile loadout could consist solely of AIM-4F SARH or AIM-4G IR Super Falcons, these missile types were usually carried in pairs.[8] As an effort to ensure the highest probability of achieving a kill, normal procedure dictated the firing of the Falcons in pairs, although it was also possible to fire all four missiles in a salvo launch against a single target. When loaded into the aircraft's weapon bay, the usual practice was to mount SARH missiles on the forward launch rails while the IR missiles were loaded on the rear rails. Since the missiles on the rear rails fired first during a multiple launch, this method prevented the heat-seeking Falcons from locking onto the heat plumes generated by the exhaust of the radar-homing missiles during their flight towards a target. Regardless of their guidance type, the Falcons were fitted with contact fuses and therefore had to strike their target in order to detonate.

The mounting of the single AIR-2A Genie missile between the rear twin launch rails caused those missiles to be positioned slightly further away from the aircraft's centerline compared to the forward missiles. Equipped with a 1.5-kiloton nuclear warhead, AIR-2A Genie was the same weapon that armed the interceptor version of the McDonnell Voodoo, the F-101B.

An F-106A on display with its armament of four AIM-4 Falcons and one AIR-2 Genie nuclear-armed rocket. (USAF)

Unlike the Falcon missiles which were lowered on launch rails when fired, the Genie was ejected from the weapons bay by a small explosive charge. After falling a short distance below the aircraft, the Genie's rocket motor fired, propelling the 9-foot long missile up to a speed of Mach 3 and to a maximum range of 6 miles. Originally, the AIR-2A was aimed using an optical sight that was installed at the top of the aircraft's windscreen, this being removed after July 1972.

As had occurred with the F-102A, the Air Force authorized the manufacture of a two-seat version of the F-106A for pilot training and proficiency purposes. This time, however, Convair decided on a tandem style seating arrangement for the trainer version of the F-106 rather than the side-by-side layout it had developed for the TF-102A. Originally designated as the TF-106A, this aircraft was redesignated as the F-106B by the USAF during August 1956 due to it retaining the full combat capability of the single-seat F-106A.[9] The first flight of the two-seat F-106B took place at Edwards Air Force Base on April 9, 1958.

Dimensionally the F-106B was identical to the F-106A,

however, the addition of a second cockpit caused some structural changes to be made to the aircraft's basic design. The placement of the rear cockpit made it necessary to move the lower electronics bay further back in the fuselage to be placed between the front two missile rails in the weapons bay.[10] Consequently, different weapon bay doors were fitted that were compatible with the revised layout. Missile carriage capability, however, was identical to that found in the F-106A. The F-106B was equipped with the AN/ASQ-25 fire control system, which was equivalent to the MA-1 installed in the single-seat aircraft, thereby providing an equal offensive capability between the two types.[11] The space taken up by the second cockpit also reduced the F-106B's internal fuel capacity to 1,450 gallons, which amounted to 64 gallons less than that of the F-106A.

The F-106B was equipped with a single piece canopy that was opened and closed by a single lowering and raising cylinder

Unlike the two-seat version of the Delta Dagger, the TF-102A, the F-106B featured a tandem cockpit arrangement. Shown here is the first production F-106B (57-2507). (USAF)

mounted just behind the forward cockpit. While parked, the large canopy was supported by a pair of tubular braces.[12] Furthermore, the canopy had a wide strip running down its center that restricted the crew's overhead visibility. This was in common with the F-106A that had also entered service with a canopy design incorporating an overhead brace. While the F-106A fleet would be retrofitted with a bubble type canopy beginning in October 1972, the two-seat F-106B retained its original canopy design throughout its career.

During its career, it was common to have a small number of F-106Bs assigned to each operational ADC and ANG F-106 squadron. Although these aircraft were generally utilized for training duties, they were routinely assigned intercept missions as well. Overall, the flight performance of the F-106B was nearly identical to that of the F-106A, with the exception that the two-seater had a slightly shorter range.

In May 1959, Convair began delivering production F-106As to the Air Defense Command at a unit cost of 4.7 million dollars apiece.[13] The first units to receive these aircraft were the 539th FIS at McGuire AFB, New Jersey, and the 498th FIS based at Geiger AFB, Washington. With the assistance of the ADC's interceptor and missile school at Tyndall AFB, Florida, the 539th FIS conducted Category III testing which concluded in early 1961.[14] Meanwhile, the 498th FIS had reached an initial operational capability with the type in October 1959. Deliveries of the F-106A concluded on July 20, 1961 when Convair delivered the last example to the Air Defense Command.[15] Including the two prototypes, 277 F-106As had been built, a far cry from the 1,000 aircraft originally envisioned by the ADC. Nonetheless, by this time, there were 14 air defense squadrons operating the F-106, which represented approximately half of the ADC's interceptor force. While in operational service, the Delta Dart's official name was rarely used as the aircraft was more commonly referred to as the "Six." It also became widely known as the "Ultimate Interceptor."

The fire-control system developed for the F-106A was the result of work by Hughes Aerospace with the MX-1179 fire-control system and digital computations for interception which dated back to 1950.[16] Designated as the MA-1, this fire-control system was integrated into NORAD's Semi-Automatic Ground Environment (SAGE) air defense system by receiving information through a Time Division Data Link (TDDL) receiver. When it was developed, SAGE represented the most advanced computer system ever created up to that time. In fact, the AN/FSQ-7 computer developed for SAGE is the largest computer known to have been built with the 54 machines constructed weighing 250 tons apiece. However, this sophisticated air defense system came with an enormous cost. It has been estimated that by time SAGE became fully deployed in 1963, some $12 billion had been spent on the project, a figure roughly equating to $88.2 billion in 2011 dollars.

While performing a typical intercept under SAGE control, the

Although generally similar in appearance to its predecessor, the F-102 Delta Dagger, the F-106 featured a squared-off vertical stabilizer, repositioned air intakes, and a superior fire-control system. (USAF)

pilot of the F-106 became something of a systems manager as he monitored the aircraft's complex electronic systems. Following takeoff, the pilot handed over control of the aircraft to the MA-1 system, which would guide it towards the target by receiving information sent by ground control stations. After reaching an offset point near the intruder, the Automatic Flight Control System (AFCS) would align the F-106 on a lead-collision or pursuit intercept course. At this point, the pilot manually locked the F-106A's onboard radar on the enemy aircraft, which would place the interceptor on a proper trajectory for weapons release by providing data to the AFCS. The MA-1 then prepared the selected armament, which was fired at the proper time when the pilot pressed the trigger. Following the engagement, SAGE provided navigational commands to the AFCS to plot a course back to base. While approaching the airfield, the F-106's automatic landing equipment would control the aircraft's descent with the pilot taking over to perform the actual landing.[17]

As could be expected from such an innovative system, the MA -1 FCS experienced severe serviceability issues during the F-106's early operational career. By early 1960, the ADC had identified 63 changes to the MA-1 and 67 airframe modifications necessary to bring early model F-106s up to the standards of the most recent examples off the assembly line. In September 1960, the USAF initiated a yearlong modification project known as Wild Goose that was intended to standardize the F-106 fleet. The majority of Wild Goose work was performed at ADC bases by teams from the Air Materiel Command working in conjunction with ADC maintenance personnel. Another improvement program, known as Broad Jump, also began in 1960 during which F-106s received further modifications at the Sacramento Air Materiel Area, which required an average of 60 days per aircraft to complete the necessary changes and was not

The cambered leading edge of the wing and the exhaust nozzle of the Pratt & Whitney J75 turbojet are visible in this view of a parked F-106A. (USAF)

completed until early 1963.[18]

During 1960, Hughes flight-tested an Infrared Search and Track (IRST) system capable of working at low altitudes and against varied backgrounds. The test results from this unit were so positive that it was quickly included in the list of F-106 improvements.[19] The IRST was installed immediately in front of the windscreen and remained retracted under a aerodynamic fairing while not in use.

In 1963, an electronic counter-countermeasures (ECCM) capability was incorporated into the MA-1 fire control system allowing it to reject radar returns generated by chaff deployed by enemy aircraft. Despite its early difficulties, the MA-1 eventually matured and following its many modifications became more dependable, although by this time the primary threat of a Soviet attack had shifted away from long-range bombers to ballistic missiles. Regardless of this, the Soviet Union still maintained a large bomber force that could not be underestimated in an age of nuclear warfare, therefore the F-106 continued to fulfill a vital role in the defense of North America.

Equipped with its powerful J75-P-17 turbojet, the F-106 had the ability to reach supersonic speeds at low altitude without the use of its afterburner, a capability commonly referred to today as supercruise.[20] The power possessed by the Delta Dart was amply demonstrated on December 15, 1959 when an F-106A (56-0467) piloted by Major Joseph Rogers set a world speed record of 1,525.96 mph at 40,500 feet.[21] Although Major Roger's record would be eclipsed a few years later by a modified US Navy F-4 Phantom II, it is still recognized as the fastest speed ever attained by a single-engine manned aircraft.

Early F-106s were equipped with an interim ejection seat produced by the Weber Aircraft Corporation, which had been derived from the seat used in the F-102 and was considered adequate for subsonic ejections only. In response, Convair developed its Rotational B ejection seat, which was designed for a survivable egress from the F-106 at supersonic speeds. Providing a safe ejection system at such speeds presented a very complex engineering problem. As can be expected, the resulting solution involved a highly complicated ejection system. This is evident in the fact that 32 separate actions were required between the pulling of the ejection handles and the first firing of a ballistic squib.[22]

Following a number of fatal ejections, the "B-seat" became very unpopular with the USAF. Furthermore, it had been determined statistically that there was a far greater chance that an ejection from an F-106 would occur at subsonic speeds rather than during supersonic flight. In 1965, to rectify this issue, the USAF issued a contract to Weber Aircraft, the producer of the interim F-106 seat, calling for the creation of a new ejection system. The resulting design was delivered to the Air Force forty -five days later and featured a true "zero-zero" (zero altitude &

zero airspeed) capability, which was verified using a human subject in 1965 during Project 90. Following the arrival of the new seats, a program to retrofit them into the ADC's F-106s began. The new Weber seat would remain in use with the Delta Dart throughout the balance of its operational career.

In May 1963, the F-106 became the first US Air Force fighter to be fitted with an arrestor hook. Designed to snag arresting wires to stop an aircraft during a runway overshoot, this device was similar in concept to those fitted to naval carrier aircraft. Although the addition of the arrestor hook became widespread during 1963, some early test installations took place during 1960-61.[23]

When the Delta Dart first entered service, it was capable of carrying a pair of 230-gallon external fuel tanks on pylons under its wings. These tanks, however, were not rated for supersonic flight, therefore restricting the F-106 to subsonic speeds while carrying them. The external tanks, however, provided a 30

A crewman services an F-106A (57-2475) belonging to the 95th FIS, which operated the Delta Dart between 1959 and 1973. (USAF)

Two F-106As fly in formation with a KC-135 Stratotanker while another is refueled. The F-106 fleet began receiving boom compatible aerial refueling receptacles in 1967. (DI)

percent increase in available fuel when compared to the F-106A's internal fuel load of 1,530 gallons.[24] In June 1967, larger 360-gallon tanks became available that were capable of being carried supersonically. The new tanks were longer and more streamlined than the earlier version making the two easily distinguishable from one another. Since the new drop tanks did not adversely affect the aircraft's performance, F-106A/Bs rarely operated without them.

When originally designed, the F-106 had no in-flight refueling capability. This was in common with its predecessor, the F-102, which only received temporary modifications to allow aerial refueling for deployment overseas. The F-106, however, was to receive a permanent in-flight refueling capability beginning in September 1967.[25] This involved the installation of a refueling receptacle at the rear of the notch on the aircraft's spine that also housed the air conditioning vent. Using this modification, the F-106 was able to replenish all of its fuel tanks, including its drop tanks, from boom equipped tanker aircraft.

The F-106 Delta Dart was the only Century Series fighter not to be involved in combat during its long career. During the Vietnam War, some consideration was given towards basing the F-106 in Southeast Asia. However, this was not to happen, and the closest the F-106 would come to combat was its deployment to South Korea beginning in February 1968 in response to the Pueblo Incident.

On January 23, 1968, North Korea seized the USS Pueblo (AGER-2), an intelligence-gathering vessel, in international waters.[26] This incident prompted the United States to undertake a major military build-up in South Korea. The first F-106 squadron to arrive in South Korea was 318th FIS when it deployed from McChord AFB to the Osan Air Base in February 1968. Over the next two years, F-106s operated from South Korea with the last unit, Dover AFB's 95th FIS, departing in May 1970.

The air war over Vietnam forced a reevaluation of the practice of not equipping US fighter aircraft with an internal gun. This, along with the F-106 having demonstrated its speed and maneuverability capabilities in the fighter versus fighter role, led to the Air Force endorsing a program to outfit the F-106A with a gun capability in 1969.[27] Known as Project Six Shooter, this modification program was slowed by technical and financial difficulties until 1972.

Six Shooter modifications included the installation of a M61A1 Vulcan cannon pod into the rear of the aircraft's weapons bay in the location formerly occupied by the AIR-2A Genie. However, the standard complement of four AIM-4F/G Falcon missiles remained unchanged. A modification to the rear of the weapon bay doors was required to allow the aerodynamic fairing of the gun pod to protrude below the aircraft.[28] While installed in the F-106A, the M61A1 20mm gun pod carried 625 rounds in its

An F-106A (59-0024) which has received Project Six Shooter modifications as evidenced by the clear top canopy and centerline gun pod. (DI)

ammunition drum and had a rate of fire of 4,500 rounds per minute.[29]

Project Six Shooter modifications also included the installation of a clear bubble type canopy. Since the original canopy had featured a wide overhead brace, this greatly improved the pilot's visibility. The first F-106A to receive Six Shooter modifications was aircraft 58-0795, while it was operating for the Air Defense Weapons Center at Tyndall AFB, Florida.[30] Only a portion of the ADC's F-106As were equipped with the gun installation, this consisting solely of aircraft that had vertical tape flight instruments. Also excluded from the program was the entire fleet of dual-place F-106Bs.

On February 2, 1970, one of the strangest incidents involving the Delta Dart took place. On this date, a flight of three F-106s of the 71st FIS departed Malmstrom AFB, Montana to conduct an Air Combat Training (ACT) exercise.[31] One of these aircraft was 58-0787, piloted by 1st Lieutenant Gary Foust. While maneuvering in mock dogfight, Foust's F-106A went into a flat spin at 35,000 feet. Despite his frantic efforts, Foust was unable to regain control of his aircraft and ejected at approximately

197

12,000 feet. In most cases, such an event leads to the destruction of the aircraft, but after Foust ejected from his F-106A it miraculously returned to straight and level flight. Meanwhile, Foust made a parachute landing into a mountainous area, later being assisted by local residents.[32]

The pilotless aircraft eventually performed a gentle belly landing in a farm field near Big Sandy, Montana. When local law enforcement officials arrived, they were surprised that the F-106A's engine was still running. An initial survey of the aircraft revealed that relatively minor damage had been suffered during the incident. A short time later, technicians from the Sacramento Air Logistics Center, McClellan AFB, arrived and partially disassembled the aircraft in order to transport it back to their facility in California by rail. Following repairs, 58-0787 returned to active duty, its final operator being the 49th FIS based at Griffiss AFB, New York. Fittingly, in August 1986, this aircraft was delivered to the National Museum of the US Air Force, where it remains on display to this day.[33]

Beginning in the mid-1960s, the changing nature of the threat posed by Soviet strategic nuclear forces caused a significant

A side view of 58-0787 after making its pilotless belly landing near Big Sandy, Montana on February 2, 1970. Today, this aircraft resides at the National Museum of the US Air Force in Dayton, Ohio. (USAF)

reduction in the size of the Air Defense Command. In 1964, there were 51 ADC squadrons and by 1968, this number had declined to just 34 units. That same year, this organization was redesignated as the Aerospace Defense Command. During the 1970s, the interception of enemy bombers became less of a priority for the USAF as it had been in the past. Accordingly, the number of F-106 units in the ADC had decreased to only six squadrons by 1976, with an additional six squadrons available from the Air National Guard. These units were complemented by a further three ANG squadrons operating the F-101B Voodoo, and two Canadian CF-101B squadrons.[34] In October 1979, the remaining USAF F-106 interceptor squadrons were transferred to the Tactical Air Command (TAC).

In April 1972, the 186th FIS of the Montana ANG became the first Guard operator of the Delta Dart. In total, the F-106 would go on to serve in 6 separate Air National Guard units between 1972 and 1988. Perhaps the most active of the Guard units were the three squadrons based along the East Coast that were often scrambled to intercept Soviet Tu-95 Bears as they made reconnaissance flights from Russia to Cuba.[35]

During the late 1970s, the USAF began phasing out the F-106 as newer aircraft such as the F-15 and F-16 entered service. Surprisingly, however, the retirement of the last F-106 squadrons in both the active duty Air Force and the Air National Guard occurred nearly simultaneously. The first National Guard unit to trade in their F-106s was the 171st FIS of the Michigan ANG, which transitioned to the F-4C Phantom II in 1978. The last active duty USAF F-106 squadron was the 49th FIS based at Griffiss AFB, which ceased operating the Delta Dart on September 30, 1987. Less than a year later, on July 7, 1988, the 119th FIS of the New Jersey ANG based at Atlantic City took their last F-106 off air defense alert, thus ending the type's 29-year career as an interceptor.

Between 1986 and 1990, eight F-106A/Bs were pressed into service as chase planes to support the B-1B bomber program. While performing in this role, these aircraft operated primarily out of Rockwell International's Palmdale, California facility, with further sorties also originating at Tinker AFB, Oklahoma. Delta Darts assigned to this program were given tail markings consisting of a silhouette of an F-106 and a B-1 flying side-by-side with their contrails combining into a pyramid shape under which was the word CHASE in a stylized font.

In July 1986, the USAF appointed Honeywell Incorporated's Defense Systems Division as the prime contractor to begin conversion of surplus F-106s into Full-Scale Aerial Targets (FSAT).[36] Designated as Pacer Six, this program called for retired F-106s to be converted into drones to serve as realistic aerial targets for training and weapon system validation purposes. Redesignated as QF-106s following conversion, this aircraft replaced the QF-100 Super Sabre as the USAF's primary target

This F-106A is pictured while operating as a chase plane during the Rockwell B-1B bomber program. (DI)

200

drone.

During the conversion process, a primary and backup Automatic Flight Control System (AFCS) was installed, along with a scoring system that had the capability to record a missile's miss distance. Among the equipment that could be employed by the QF-106 during a mission were chaff/flare dispensers, infrared pods, and a smoke system.[37]

The QF-106 went airborne for the first time in July 1987. As was the case with the QF-102, droned Delta Darts operated out of Holloman AFB, New Mexico and Tyndall AFB, Florida over the White Sands Missile and Eglin Gulf Test Ranges respectively. Final QF-106 deliveries took place in late 1994, after at least 181 had been rebuilt with each conversion costing approximately $250,000.[38] The last destruction of a QF-106 drone occurred over New Mexico on February 20, 1997. Following the conclusion of QF-106 operations, the FSAT role was assumed by the QF-4 Phantom II.

The Delta Dart's superb performance capabilities made it an attractive test platform for NASA, which used a handful of F-106s in a variety of experimental programs. In 1966, an F-106B, 57-2516, was acquired by that agency for use in research work concerning the US supersonic transport (SST) program. Following it entering the NASA fleet, it was assigned the civil registration N616NA (616) and operated out of the Lewis Research Center at Cleveland, Ohio. In January 1979, this aircraft was transferred to NASA's Dryden Flight Research Center at Edwards AFB and redesignated as N816NA (816). Number 816 was subsequently loaned to the Langley Research Center where it was modified to take part in NASA's Storm Hazards Research Program, during which it would be purposely flown into thunderstorms to be struck by lightning. While involved in this project, this aircraft recorded being struck by lightning 714 times during 1,496 thunderstorm penetrations, thus providing valuable information on the behavior of thunderstorms and the effects of lightning strikes on modern aircraft. In May 1991, N816NA was retired by NASA, and subsequently placed on display at the Virginia Air & Space Center.

Meanwhile, another F-106B, 57-2507, was acquired by NASA in 1972. Following its acquisition, this aircraft was reregistered as N607NA (607) and was employed in numerous projects prior to being reduced to a non-flyable status in 1984. While operating for NASA, F-106Bs were assigned the NF-106B designation to reflect their new role as research aircraft.

In 1997, NASA's Dryden Flight Research Center became involved in a joint endeavor by the USAF and Kelly Space and Technology Incorporated known as the Eclipse project. The goal of this project was to study the feasibility of towing a reusable space launch vehicle behind a conventional aircraft to high-altitude prior to the ignition of its own engines to propel it into low-earth orbit. To support the program, two QF-106 drones, 59-0010 & 59-0130, were selected as candidates for conversion into piloted experimental aircraft. One of these, 59-0130, was selected as the primary aircraft and converted at Dryden into the EXD-01 (Eclipse Experimental Demonstrator-01).[39] Among the modification work performed was the shortening of the nose pitot boom, and the installation of a towrope attachment and release mechanism just in front of the aircraft's windscreen.

On December 20, 1997, the flight test portion of the Eclipse project began when a C-141 Starlifter pulled a tethered QF-106 (EXD-01) into the skies above Edwards AFB. Of the two QF-106s selected for the program, only 59-0130 actually participated in the flight tests, the other serving as a backup aircraft. During these flights, the QF-106 would be towed to an altitude of approximately 20,000 feet before the tether was released, allowing the pilot to perform a conventional landing. Eclipse test flights concluded on February 6, 1998 following the sixth and

The EXD-01 (59-0130) is pulled aloft on its first tethered flight. (NASA)

final flight of the program. Following the conclusion of the Eclipse project, the two QF-106s involved in the program arrived at Davis-Monthan AFB for storage at the Aerospace Maintenance and Regeneration Center (AMARC).

Beginning in the late 1950s, a number of advanced F-106 variants were offered to the Air Force, one such example being the F-106C/D. This proposed model incorporated a 40-inch parabolic radar antenna, as opposed to the standard 23-inch antenna installed in the F-106A. To support this program's development, a pair of F-106As, 57-0239 & 57-0240, received modifications to evaluate the proposal. The installation of the larger radar dish required the fitting of an enlarged radome that resulted in a 5-foot extension of the nose. It also required a reworking of the fuselage aft of the radome split line to a point just in front of the engine air intakes. Only aircraft 57-0239 was used to perform test flights in the new configuration, while 57-0240 was utilized strictly as a radar system testbed.[40]

During the spring of 1959, the modified F-106A performed ten test flights. These flights revealed that the larger nosecone and fuselage alterations had no adverse effect upon the aircraft's performance. In fact, pilots flying the modified plane reported that the handling characteristics were virtually indistinguishable from those possessed by a standard F-106A.[41] In the end, however, the Air Force did not proceed forward with the project.

Along with the F-105 Thunderchief, the F-106 Delta Dart was the only other Century Series fighter not exported to any foreign users. Following the Canadian government's decision to cancel the Avro Arrow project in February 1959, some consideration was given towards acquiring the F-106C/D to fill that nation's interceptor requirement. In the end, however, it would be McDonnell's F-101B Voodoo that was selected to fill this role.

During its production run, Convair produced 340 Delta Darts, of which 277 were F-106As while 63 additional aircraft were two-seat F-106Bs.[42] The F-106 was the Air Force's first fighter aircraft to serve over twenty years in frontline service. The F-106 also proved to be the final dedicated jet interceptor to be built for the Air Force. Despite the USAF conducting studies during the 1960s to develop an advanced interceptor aircraft, no successor to the Delta Dart was ever fielded, thus the F-106 served through most of the Cold War as America's primary jet interceptor.

Being the last of the Century Series fighters to enter service, it is not surprising that the type's retirement in 1988 signified the final chapter in the active-duty history of this class of fighters with the USAF. Today, there are at least 23 examples of the Delta Dart preserved in museums around the United States.

# NOTES

## Introduction

1.  Bill Gunston. *Air Power, A Modern Illustrated Military History*, p. 142-143.
2.  Steve Pace. *X-Fighters*, p. 13-15.
3.  Iblid, p. 15.
4.  Ilbid, p. 17.
5.  Bill Gunston. *The Illustrated History of Fighters*, p. 147.
6.  Lawrence R. Benson & Karen Pittman. *Sabre to Stealth*, p. 12.
7.  The Soviet Union's development of nuclear weapons benefited greatly from espionage efforts directed against the US atomic bomb program.
8.  Bill Gunston. *The Illustrated History of Fighters*, p. 157.
9.  National Museum of the US Air Force. *Technical Notes: North American F-86A Sabre.*
10. Peter March. *Sabre to Stealth*, p. 24.
11. Jim Winchester. *Fighter*, p. 183.
12. Soviet pilots also participated in the air war over Korea, a fact not confirmed until the end of the Cold War.
13. The delivery of nuclear weapons by bomber aircraft remains a cornerstone of the nuclear deterrence capability of the United States.
14. William Green. *Famous Fighters of the Second World War*, p. 91.

## Chapter 1
### North American F-100 Super Sabre

1.  Steve Pace. *X-Fighters*, p. 106-107.
2.  The F-86D Sabre was an all-weather interceptor version of the Sabre family. Fitted with a nose radar unit and a belly mounted rocket pack, its primary mission was to intercept enemy bombers.
3.  Steve Pace. *X-Fighters*, p. 109.
4.  Iblid, p. 109.
5.  Marcelle Size Knaack. *Encyclopedia of US Air Force Aircraft & Missile Systems, Volume 1*, p. 113-4.
6.  United States Air Force. *Standard Aircraft Characteristics, YF-100, Service Test , May 1953.*
7.  The term Florida Panhandle is an unofficial geographic term used to describe the northwestern region of the state of Florida.

8.  Hill AFB Fact Sheet. *20mm Revolving Cannon, Pontiac M39A3 20mm Revolving Cannon.*
9.  Marcelle Size Knaack. *Encyclopedia of US Air Force Aircraft & Missile Systems, Volume 1,* p. 115.
10. Iblid, p. 115-116.
11. Steve Pace. *X-Fighters,* p. 110.
12. Thomas E. Gardner. *F-100 Super Sabre At War,* p. 41.
13. William Green. *The World's Fighting Planes,* p. 207.
14. Marcelle Size Knaack. *Encyclopedia of US Air Force Aircraft & Missile Systems, Volume 1,* p. 116.
15. United States Air Force. *Standard Aircraft Characteristics, F-100A, January 1961.*
16. Thomas E. Gardner. *F-100 Super Sabre At War,* p. 98.
17. William Green. *The World's Fighting Planes,* p. 207.
18. Marcelle Size Knaack. *Encyclopedia of US Air Force Aircraft & Missile Systems, Volume 1,* p. 118.
19. U. S. Air Force Fact Sheet. *Technical notes for the F-100C.*
20. Marcelle Size Knaack. *Encyclopedia of US Air Force Aircraft & Missile Systems, Volume 1,* p. 120.
21. William Green. *The World's Fighting Planes,* p. 208.
22. Marcelle Size Knaack. *Encyclopedia of US Air Force Aircraft & Missile Systems, Volume 1,* p. 123-124.
23. Thomas E. Gardner. *F-100 Super Sabre At War,* p. 70.
24. Marcelle Size Knaack. *Encyclopedia of US Air Force Aircraft & Missile Systems, Volume 1,* p. 124.
25. Iblid, p. 129.
26. William Green. *The World's Fighting Planes,* p. 208.
27. U. S. Air Force Fact Sheet. *Technical notes for the F-100F.*
28. Due to an energy crisis, the Thunderbirds flew the T-38 Talon trainer from 1974 to 1982.
29. Rebecca Grant. *Victor Alert, Air Force Magazine,* March 2011, Vol. 94 No. 3.
30. James Gibson. *The History of the US Nuclear Arsenal,* p. 84.
31. Marcelle Size Knaack. *Encyclopedia of US Air Force Aircraft & Missile Systems, Volume 1,* p. 133.
32. Warren E. Thompson. *Victor Alert, Combat Aircraft,* Vol. 3 No. 4, p. 377.
33. Iblid, p. 377.
34. Thomas E. Gardner. *F-100 Super Sabre At War,* p. 123-124.
35. Robert Dorr. *History in Blue, Mock attack turned real, tragic in 1961, Air Force Times,* December 22, 2003.

36. Marcelle Size Knaack. *Encyclopedia of US Air Force Aircraft & Missile Systems, Volume 1*, p. 126.
37. US Air Force Fact Sheet. *F-100 Super Sabre in Southeast Asia.*
38. Air Force Magazine. *Up From Kitty Hawk Chronology, 1965.*
39. Iblid.
40. Bernard C. Nalty. *The Vietnam War*, p.88.
41. Lon O. Nordeen. *Air Warfare in the Missile Age*, p. 5.
42. Larry Davis. *Wild Weasel*, p. 8.
43. Iblid, p. 8.
44. Iblid, p. 8-10
45. Lt. Colonel Allen Lamb. *The First Wild Weasel and The First Wild Weasel SAM Kill, Friends Journal*, Air Force Museum Foundation, Vol. 28 No. 3, Fall 2005, p. 5-6.
46. Larry Davis. *Wild Weasel*, p. 13.
47. National Museum of the US Air Force Fact Sheet. *F-100 Super Sabre in Southeast Asia.*
48. Bill Gunston. *Modern Military Aircraft*, p. 90.
49. William Green. *The World's Fighting Planes*, p. 208.
50. Thomas E. Gardner. *F-100 Super Sabre At War*, p. 80.
51. Chris Bishop, Editor. *The Encyclopedia of 20th Century Air Warfare*, p. 462.
52. Thomas E. Gardner. *F-100 Super Sabre At War*, p. 77.
53. Iblid, p. 105.
54. US Air Force. *Official USAF F-100 Accident Rate Table.*

# Chapter 2
## McDonnell F-101 Voodoo

1. Steve Pace. *X-Fighters*, p. 71.
2. René J. Francillon. *McDonnell Douglas Aircraft since 1920, Volume II*, p. 110.
3. Iblid, p. 110-111.
4. Steve Pace. *X-Fighters*, p. 73.
5. René J. Francillon. *McDonnell Douglas Aircraft since 1920, Volume II*, p. 111.
6. Steve Pace. *X-Fighters*, p. 72.
7. René J. Francillon. *McDonnell Douglas Aircraft since 1920, Volume II*, p. 112-113.
8. Steve Pace. *X-Fighters*, p. 74.

9.  Michael J. H. Taylor & John W. R. Taylor. *Jane's Research and Experimental Aircraft*, p. 141.
10. NACA Research Memorandum, *RM L57E20*, July 10, 1957.
11. Steve Pace. *X-Fighters*, p. 75.
12. Marcelle Size Knaack. *Encyclopedia of US Air Force Aircraft & Missile Systems, Volume 1*, p. 136.
13. Iblid, p. 137.
14. René J. Francillon. *McDonnell Douglas Aircraft since 1920, Volume II*, p. 139.
15. Iblid, p. 141.
16. Marcelle Size Knaack. *Encyclopedia of US Air Force Aircraft & Missile Systems, Volume 1*, p. 138.
17. Iblid, p. 138.
18. Iblid, p. 139.
19. Iblid, p. 140.
20. USAF Standard Aircraft Characteristics. *F-101A Nov. 1962 & F-100A Jan 61, Loading and Performance – Typical Mission*.
21. Walter J. Boyne. *Airpower Classics, F/RF-101 Voodoo*, Air Force Magazine, May 2008.
22. Robert Jackson. *Modern Military Aircraft*, p. 235.
23. National Museum of the U. S. Air Force Fact Sheet. *Technical Notes (F-101A, Block 25 and later)*.
24. René J. Francillon. *McDonnell Douglas Aircraft since 1920, Volume II*, p. 142.
25. USAF Standard Aircraft Characteristics. *F-101A Nov. 1962*.
26. Marcelle Size Knaack. *Encyclopedia of US Air Force Aircraft & Missile Systems, Volume 1*, p. 141.
27. Iblid, 141-142.
28. René J. Francillon. *McDonnell Douglas Aircraft since 1920, Volume II*, p. 143.
29. USAF Standard Aircraft Characteristics. *F-101A Nov. 1962, F-101C Sep. 1958, RF-101A May 1957*.
30. Marcelle Size Knaack. *Encyclopedia of US Air Force Aircraft & Missile Systems, Volume 1*, p. 143.
31. Iblid, p. 143.
32. Iblid, p. 144-145.
33. Iblid, p. 145-146.
34. National Museum of the US Air Force. *Operation Sun Run Fact Sheet*.
35. René J. Francillon. *McDonnell Douglas Aircraft since 1920, Volume II*, p. 151.
36. Dick van der Aart. *Aerial Espionage*, p. 37-38.

37. The fact that the United States had positioned nuclear-armed Jupiter ballistic missiles in Turkey compelled the Soviet Union in adopting a similar doctrine in regards to Cuba.
38. Dick van der Aart. *Aerial Espionage*, p. 38.
39. Air Force Magazine. *Up From Kitty Hawk Chronology, 1962.*
40. Michael Dobbs. *One Minute to Midnight*, p. 178.
41. Peter March. *Sabre to Stealth*, p. 60.
42. William H. Greenhalg. *The Air Force in Southeast Asia, The RF-101 Voodoo 1961-1970*, p. 26-29.
43. Iblid, p. 31-32.
44. Peter March. *Sabre to Stealth*, p. 66.
45. William H. Greenhalg. *The Air Force in Southeast Asia, The RF-101 Voodoo 1961-1970*, p. 71-72.
46. Iblid, 108-109.
47. Marcelle Size Knaack. *Encyclopedia of US Air Force Aircraft & Missile Systems, Volume 1*, p. 149.
48. René J. Francillon. *McDonnell Douglas Aircraft since 1920, Volume II*, p. 154.
49. Iblid, p. 150.
50. Iblid, p. 154.
51. Tony Buttler. *American Secret Projects, Fighters and Interceptors 1945-1978*, P. 54.
52. Marcelle Size Knaack. *Encyclopedia of US Air Force Aircraft & Missile Systems, Volume 1*, p. 150-151.
53. René J. Francillon. *McDonnell Douglas Aircraft since 1920, Volume II*, p. 145.
54. USAF Standard Aircraft Characteristics. *F-101A Nov. 1962, F-101B Sep. 1958, F-101C Sep. 1958.*
55. Marcelle Size Knaack. *Encyclopedia of US Air Force Aircraft & Missile Systems, Volume 1*, p. 151-152.
56. USAF Standard Aircraft Characteristics. *F-101B Sep. 1958.*
57. Boeing. *MB-1/AIR-2 Genie Missile History.*
58. The Genie's only live firing test took place on July 19, 1957 over Yucca Flats, Nevada.
59. Marcelle Size Knaack. *Encyclopedia of US Air Force Aircraft & Missile Systems, Volume 1*, p. 152.
60. Iblid, p. 153.
61. René J. Francillon. *McDonnell Douglas Aircraft since 1920, Volume II*, p. 148.
62. Marcelle Size Knaack. *Encyclopedia of US Air Force Aircraft & Missile Systems, Volume 1*, p. 154.

63. René J. Francillon. *McDonnell Douglas Aircraft since 1920, Volume II*, p. 154-155.
64. The Royal Canadian Air Force became integrated into a combined military structure known as the Canadian Armed Forces in 1968. The air arm of this structure was redesignated as Air Command in 1975. In August 2011, the Canadian government announced that the nation's air force would once again be designated as the Royal Canadian Air Force (RCAF).
65. René J. Francillon. *McDonnell Douglas Aircraft since 1920, Volume II*, p. 147.
66. David L. Bashow. *On through the Hail!, The Story of the Canadian CF-18 Hornet*, Airpower, March 1987, p. 24-33.
67. René J. Francillon. *McDonnell Douglas Aircraft since 1920*, p. 147 & 156.

# Chapter 3
## Convair F-102 Delta Dagger

1. Bill Gunston. *Fighters of the Fifties*, p. 21.
2. Paul Eden. *The Encyclopedia of Aircraft of WWII*, p. 352-353.
3. In 1958, NACA was superseded by the National Aeronautics and Space Administration (NASA).
4. Steve Pace. *X-Fighters*, p. 89
5. Tony Buttler. *American Secret Projects Fighters and Interceptors 1945-1978*, p. 24.
6. Steve Pace. *X-Fighters*, p. 91.
7. National Museum of the USAF Fact Sheet. *Convair XF-92A.*
8. While being flown by Chuck Yeager in a dive, the XF-92A reached a speed of Mach 1.10. This is the only known occasion that the Dart exceeded the speed of sound.
9. While relating strategic strike capabilities, particularly during the early days of the Cold War, it was common for references to describe the offensive range capabilities of Soviet bombers in terms of one-way missions.
10. Marcelle Size Knaack. *Encyclopedia of US Air Force Aircraft & Missile Systems, Volume 1*, p. 159.
11. Iblid, p. 159-160.
12. Today, this same concept is used to lower a stealth aircraft's radar cross-section.

13. Although losing out to Convair, Republic was permitted to continue development work on the XF-103 until the USAF terminated the program on August 21, 1957.
14. Marcelle Size Knaack. *Encyclopedia of US Air Force Aircraft & Missile Systems, Volume 1,* p. 160.
15. Iblid, p. 163.
16. Iblid, p. 162.
17. Iblid, p. 163.
18. Steve Pace. *X-Fighters,* p. 121.
19. Marcelle Size Knaack. *Encyclopedia of US Air Force Aircraft & Missile Systems, Volume 1,* p. 163.
20. Steve Pace. *X-Fighters,* p. 121.
21. Larry Davis. *F-102A Delta Dagger in action,* p. 11.
22. Iblid, p. 11.
23. Marcelle Size Knaack. *Encyclopedia of US Air Force Aircraft & Missile Systems, Volume 1,* p. 164.
24. Larry Davis. *F-102A Delta Dagger in action,* p. 11.
25. Iblid, p. 11.
26. Walter J. Boyne. *Airpower Classics, F-102 Delta Dagger,* Air Force Magazine, July 2010.
27. Marcelle Size Knaack. *Encyclopedia of US Air Force Aircraft & Missile Systems, Volume 1,* p. 166.
28. Bill Gunston. Fighters of the Fifties, p. 25.
29. Marcelle Size Knaack. *Encyclopedia of US Air Force Aircraft & Missile Systems, Volume 1,* p. 165-166.
30. Larry Davis. *F-102A Delta Dagger in action,* p. 20.
31. Marcelle Size Knaack. *Encyclopedia of US Air Force Aircraft & Missile Systems, Volume 1,* p. 162.
32. Wayne Mutza. *Convair F-102 Delta Dagger,* p. 38.
33. Larry Davis. *F-102A Delta Dagger in action,* p. 18.
34. Marcelle Size Knaack. *Encyclopedia of US Air Force Aircraft & Missile Systems, Volume 1,* p. 167.
35. Wayne Mutza. *Convair F-102 Delta Dagger,* p. 21-22.
36. Marcelle Size Knaack. *Encyclopedia of US Air Force Aircraft & Missile Systems, Volume 1,* p. 171.
37. Wayne Mutza. *Convair F-102 Delta Dagger,* p. 24.
38. USAF Standard Aircraft Characteristics. *TF-102A Mar. 1956.*
39. Wayne Mutza. *Convair F-102 Delta Dagger,* p. 24-25.
40. Marcelle Size Knaack. *Encyclopedia of US Air Force Aircraft & Missile Systems, Volume 1,* p. 172.
41. Iblid, p. 171.

42. Iblid, p. 172.
43. Larry Davis. *F-102A Delta Dagger in action*, p. 40.
44. Iblid, p. 18.
45. Alaska did not receive statehood until 1959.
46. Larry Davis. *F-102A Delta Dagger in action*, p. 18.
47. Iblid, p. 20.
48. Marcelle Size Knaack. *Encyclopedia of US Air Force Aircraft & Missile Systems, Volume 1*, p. 166.
49. Wayne Mutza. *Convair F-102 Delta Dagger*, p. 69.
50. J. D. Ragay. *F-102 Delta Dagger in Europe*, p. 3.
51. Iblid, p. 6.
52. Wheelus Airbase, now known as the Mitiga International Airport is located just east of Tripoli. Beginning during the mid-1950s, Wheelus served as a major training facility for the USAFE, prior to US forces leaving Libya in 1970.
53. J. D. Ragay. *F-102 Delta Dagger in Europe*, p. 10.
54. Iblid, p. 58.
55. Larry Davis. *F-102A Delta Dagger in action*, p. 23.
56. Iblid, p. 23.
57. Iblid, p. 23.
58. Wayne Mutza. *Convair F-102 Delta Dagger*, p. 95.
59. Larry Davis. *F-102A Delta Dagger in action*, p. 29.
60. Wayne Mutza. *Convair F-102 Delta Dagger*, p. 87-89.
61. Larry Davis. *F-102A Delta Dagger in action*, p. 33.
62. Wayne Mutza. *Convair F-102 Delta Dagger*, p. 97.
63. Marcelle Size Knaack. *Encyclopedia of US Air Force Aircraft & Missile Systems, Volume 1*, p. 170.
64. Wayne Mutza. *Convair F-102 Delta Dagger*, p. 132.
65. To this day, the actual outcome of this engagement is disputed. However, most sources indicate that the Hellenic fighters were victorious.

## Chapter 4
### Lockheed F-104 Starfighter

1. William T. Y'Blood. *MiG Alley, The Fight For Air Superiority*, p. 44.
2. James Jabara. *A Fighter Pilot's Airplane*, Air Force Magazine, August 1960, p. 60.
3. Bill Gunston. *American Warplanes*, p. 122.
4. Bill Gunston. *Fighters of the Fifties*, p. 120-121.

5. Marcelle Size Knaack. *Encyclopedia of US Air Force Aircraft & Missile Systems, Volume 1*, p. 175.
6. Some sources refer to Lockheed's design as being designated the CL-246.
7. Marcelle Size Knaack. *Encyclopedia of US Air Force Aircraft & Missile Systems, Volume 1*, p. 176.
8. Michael J. H. Taylor & John W. R. Taylor. *Jane's Pocket Book 12, Research and Experimental Aircraft*, p. 81.
9. Marcelle Size Knaack. *Encyclopedia of US Air Force Aircraft & Missile Systems, Volume 1*, p. 175.
10. *The World's Greatest Aircraft*, p. 163.
11. Iblid, p. 163.
12. Tony Buttler. *American Secret Projects Fighters and Interceptors 1945-1978*, p. 75.
13. Steve Pace. *X-Fighters*, p. 130.
14. Iblid, p. 130
15. The fact that the XF-104's downward firing ejection seats were unusable at low altitudes, deserves due consideration.
16. Marcelle Size Knaack. *Encyclopedia of US Air Force Aircraft & Missile Systems, Volume 1*, p. 177.
17. Steve Pace. *X-Fighters*, p. 131.
18. *The World's Greatest Aircraft*, p. 163.
19. Marcelle Size Knaack. *Encyclopedia of US Air Force Aircraft & Missile Systems, Volume 1*, p. 177.
20. Bill Gunston. *Fighters of the Fifties*, p. 122.
21. Steve Pace. *X-Fighters*, p. 131.
22. Bill Gunston. *Fighters of the Fifties*, p. 122.
23. A deep stall is also referred to as a super-stall.
24. Marcelle Size Knaack. *Encyclopedia of US Air Force Aircraft & Missile Systems, Volume 1*, p. 177.
25. Iblid, p. 178.
26. Bill Gunston. *Fighters of the Fifties*, p. 122.
27. Peter March. *Sabre to Stealth*, p. 48.
28. Marcelle Size Knaack. *Encyclopedia of US Air Force Aircraft & Missile Systems, Volume 1*, p. 177.
29. William Green. *The World's Fighting Planes*, p. 176.
30. National Museum of the US Air Force. *Lockheed XF-104 to F-104A Fact Sheet*.
31. Michael J. H. & John W. R. Taylor. *Missiles of the World*, p. 133.
32. Ray Bonds. *The Modern US War Machine*, p. 228-229.

33. Marcelle Size Knaack. *Encyclopedia of US Air Force Aircraft & Missile Systems, Volume 1*, p. 181.

34. The Quemoy Crisis is also known as the Second Taiwan Strait Crisis.

35. John G. Norris. *Starfighters on Formosa*, Air Force Magazine, January 1959, p. 101-104.

36. Marcelle Size Knaack. *Encyclopedia of US Air Force Aircraft & Missile Systems, Volume 1*, p. 179-180.

37. Iblid, p. 180.

38. Iblid, p. 180.

39. USAF Standard Aircraft Characteristics. *F-104C Starfighter, Dec. 1958.*

40. Marcelle Size Knaack. *Encyclopedia of US Air Force Aircraft & Missile Systems, Volume 1*, p. 182.

41. USAF Standard Aircraft Characteristics. *F-104C Starfighter, Dec. 1958.*

42. Marcelle Size Knaack. *Encyclopedia of US Air Force Aircraft & Missile Systems, Volume 1*, p. 182.

43. Iblid, 183.

44. The Big Eye Task Force was redesignated as the College Eye Task Force in March 1967 following its relocation to Ubon RTAB, Thailand.

45. Bernard C. Nalty. *Tactics and Techniques of Electronic Warfare, Electronic Countermeasures in the Air War Against North Vietnam 1965-1973*, p. 126.

46. Tom Delashaw & Mark Bovankovich. *USAF Starfighters over Vietnam.*

47. Two of these losses were to AAA fire while another was downed by a SAM.

48. The Canadair Sabre was a license built version of North American Aviation's F-86 Sabre.

49. *The World's Greatest Aircraft*, p. 165.

50. Iblid, p. 165.

51. William Green. *The World's Fighting Planes*, p. 178-179.

52. Iblid, p. 182.

53. Marcelle Size Knaack. *Encyclopedia of US Air Force Aircraft & Missile Systems, Volume 1*, p. 185.

54. Bill Gunston & Mike Spick. *Modern Air Combat*, p. 116.

55. William Green. *The World's Fighting Planes*, p. 179.

56. Iblid, p. 179-180.

57. *The World's Greatest Aircraft*, p. 166.

58. Bill Gunston & Mike Spick. *Modern Air Combat*, p. 116.

59. Some RF-104Gs were subsequently modified to F-104G standards after becoming no longer needed for reconnaissance duties.

60. Lt. Colonel Frank H. Robertson. *Military Assistance Training Program*, Air University Review, September-October 1968.

61. Bill Gunston. *Fighters of the Fifties*, p. 125.

62. Walter J. Boyne. *Airpower Classics,* Air Force Magazine, February 2008, p. 88.
63. *The World's Greatest Aircraft,* p. 166.
64. Alfred Price. *Air Battle Central Europe,* p. 140-147.
65. William Green. *The World's Fighting Planes,* p. 11.
66. Iblid, p. 11.
67. Iblid, P. 11.
68. The Royal Canadian Air Force became integrated into a combined military structure known as the Canadian Armed Forces in 1968. The air arm of this structure was redesignated as Air Command in 1975. In August 2011, the Canadian government announced that the nation's air force would once again be designated as the Royal Canadian Air Force (RCAF).
69. Bill Gunston. *Modern Military Aircraft,* p. 80.
70. René J. Francillon. *Naval Institute Guide to World Military Aviation 1995,* p. 528.
71. Due to the crash of one aircraft during a test flight, the total number of F-104Ss built was 246.
72. William Green. *The World's Fighting Planes,* p. 179.
73. Iblid, p. 182.
74. Walter J. Boyne. *Airpower Classics, F-104 Starfighter,* Air Force Magazine, February 2008, p. 88.
75. Phillip Friddell. *F-104 Starfighter in Action,* p. 9.
76. Lon O. Nordeen. *Air Warfare in the Missile Age,* p.73.
77. Iblid, p. 66-67.
78. Iblid, p. 76.
79. The Soviet K-13 (AA-2 Atoll) was a reverse engineered copy of the US AIM-9 Sidewinder.
80. Lon O. Nordeen. *Air Warfare in the Missile Age,* p. 82-83.
81. Steven Siceloff. *Starfighters Ready to Launch Research, Satellites,* Kennedy Space Center News, 5-20-2011.
82. Tony Buttler. *American Secret Projects Fighters and Interceptors 1945-1978,* p. 195.

# Chapter 5
## Republic F-105 Thunderchief

1. Originally entered into the competition as the two-seat SEV-2XP, this aircraft was subsequently modified into a single seat fighter with retractable landing gear and redesignated as the SEV-1XP.

2. Bill Gunston. *American Warplanes*, p. 66.
3. Iblid, p. 77.
4. Paul Eden. *Encyclopedia of Aircraft of World War II*, p. 428.
5. Bill Gunston. *American Warplanes*, p. 118.
6. David Anderton. *Republic F-105 Thunderchief*, p. 16.
7. Iblid, p. 18.
8. Bill Gunston. *Fighters of the Fifties*, p. 195.
9. Marcelle Size Knaack. *Encyclopedia of US Air Force Aircraft & Missile Systems, Volume 1*, p. 191
10. Iblid, p. 191.
11. Iblid, p. 191.
12. David Anderton. *Republic F-105 Thunderchief*, p. 19.
13. Marcelle Size Knaack. *Encyclopedia of US Air Force Aircraft & Missile Systems, Volume 1*, p. 191-192.
14. David Anderton. *Republic F-105 Thunderchief*, p. 21.
15. Iblid, p. 31-32.
16. Iblid, p. 40.
17. Ken Nuebeck. *F-105 Thunderchief in action*, p. 9.
18. David Anderton. *Republic F-105 Thunderchief*, p. 42.
19. Ken Nuebeck. *F-105 Thunderchief in action*, p. 8.
20. Iblid, p. 8.
21. United States Air Force. *Standard Aircraft Characteristics, F-105B-10*, 17 October 1958.
22. Marcelle Size Knaack. *Encyclopedia of US Air Force Aircraft & Missile Systems, Volume 1*, p. 193.
23. Ken Nuebeck. *F-105 Thunderchief in action*, p. 8.
24. Marcelle Size Knaack. *Encyclopedia of US Air Force Aircraft & Missile Systems, Volume 1*, p. 193.
25. Ken Nuebeck. *F-105 Thunderchief in action*, p. 9.
26. Iblid, p. 15.
27. US Air Force. *Standard Aircraft Characteristics, F-105D-31*, June 1970.
28. David Anderton. *Republic F-105 Thunderchief*, p. 65-66.
29. Iblid, p. 68.
30. Marcelle Size Knaack. *Encyclopedia of US Air Force Aircraft & Missile Systems, Volume 1*, p. 196.
31. Iblid, p. 196.
32. Ken Nuebeck. *F-105 Thunderchief in action*, p. 31.
33. United States Air Force. *Characteristics Summary, F-105D-31, January 1964*.
34. Marcelle Size Knaack. *Encyclopedia of US Air Force Aircraft & Missile Systems, Volume 1*, p. 197-198.

35. David Anderton. *Republic F-105 Thunderchief*, p. 80.
36. Marcelle Size Knaack. *Encyclopedia of US Air Force Aircraft & Missile Systems, Volume 1*, p. 198.
37. Ken Nuebeck. *F-105 Thunderchief in action*, p. 17.
38. Larry Davis. *'Thuds' and Weasels, The F-105 in SEA, 1964-1974, Wings of Fame, Volume 18*, p. 17.
39. Iblid, p. 21.
40. Ken Nuebeck. *F-105 Thunderchief in action*, p. 42
41. David Anderton. *Republic F-105 Thunderchief*, p. 118-119. *(Note: Some sources suggest that the missile was actually a Soviet built Atoll.)*
42. Ken Nuebeck. *F-105 Thunderchief in action*, p. 42.
43. Lou Drendel. *...And Kill MiGs*, p. 47.
44. Fairchild Hiller acquired Republic Aviation in 1965.
45. Theodore Van Geffen, Jr. & Gerald C. Arruda. *Thuderchief*, Air University Review, January-February 1983.
46. David Anderton. *Republic F-105 Thunderchief*, p. 184.
47. Iblid, p. 184.
48. Marcelle Size Knaack. *Encyclopedia of US Air Force Aircraft & Missile Systems, Volume 1*, p. 201.
49. John W. R. Taylor & Gordon Swanborough. *Military Aircraft of the World*, p. 222.
50. Ken Nuebeck. *F-105 Thunderchief in action*, p. 32.
51. Marcelle Size Knaack. *Encyclopedia of US Air Force Aircraft & Missile Systems, Volume 1*, p. 202.
52. Michael J. H. & John W. R. Taylor. *Missiles of the World*, p. 132.
53. Marcelle Size Knaack. *Encyclopedia of US Air Force Aircraft & Missile Systems, Volume 1*, p. 202.
54. Larry Davis. *'Thuds' and Weasels, The F-105 in SEA, 1964-1974, Wings of Fame, Volume 18*, p. 27-28.
55. Ken Nuebeck. *F-105 Thunderchief in action*, p. 35.
56. Iblid, p. 35.
57. Larry Davis. *'Thuds' and Weasels, The F-105 in SEA, 1964-1974, Wings of Fame, Volume 18*, p. 34.
58. Iblid, p. 28.
59. David Anderton. *Republic F-105 Thunderchief*, p. 186.
60. MASDC was later redesignated as Aerospace Maintenance and Regeneration Center (AMARC) in 1985. Since 2007, it has been designated as the 309th Aerospace Maintenance and Regeneration Group (AMARG).

# Chapter 6
## Convair F-106 Delta Dart

1. Steve Pace. *X-Fighters*, p. 76.
2. Marcelle Size Knaack. *Encyclopedia of US Air Force Aircraft & Missile Systems, Volume 1*, p. 208-209.
3. Iblid, p. 209.
4. Bert Kinzey. *F-106 Delta Dart*, p. 6.
5. Marcelle Size Knaack. *Encyclopedia of US Air Force Aircraft & Missile Systems, Volume 1*, p. 210.
6. Bert Kinzey. *F-106 Delta Dart*, p. 6.
7. The F-102A had a maximum gross weight of 31,276 pounds. (*USAF Standard Aircraft Characteristics, F-102A, August 1962.*)
8. Prior to 1963, the AIM-4F and AIM-4G had been designated as the GAR-3A and GAR-4A respectively.
9. Marcelle Size Knaack. *Encyclopedia of USAF Aircraft & Missile Systems, Volume 1*, p. 219.
10. Bert Kinzey. *F-106 Delta Dart*, p. 62.
11. Marcelle Size Knaack. *Encyclopedia of US Air Force Aircraft & Missile Systems, Volume 1*, p. 219.
12. Don Carson & Lou Drendel. *F-106 Delta Dart in Action*, p. 6.
13. Ray Wagner. *American Combat Planes*, p. 473.
14. Marcelle Size Knaack. *Encyclopedia of US Air Force Aircraft & Missile Systems, Volume 1*, p. 213.
15. William Green. *The World's Fighting Planes*, p. 138.
16. Air Force Systems Command. *Development of Airborne Armament 1910-1961, Volume IV, Advanced Intercept Fire Control*, p. 591.
17. Iblid, p. 593-596.
18. Marcelle Size Knaack. *Encyclopedia of US Air Force Aircraft & Missile Systems, Volume 1*, p. 213-214.
19. Iblid, p. 214.
20. Walter J. Boyne. *Airpower Classics*, Air Force Magazine, November 2009, p. 80.
21. The F-106A originally intended to make the record attempt, 56-0459, experienced technical problems, which led to the use of a backup aircraft, 56-0467.
22. Col. Jack Broughton. *F-106 Delta Dart*, Combat Aircraft, April-May 2009, p. 72.
23. Bert Kinzey. *F-106 Delta Dart*, p. 11.

24. US Air Force. *Standard Aircraft Characteristics, F-106A Delta Dart, October 1961.*

25. Bert Kinzey. *F-106 Delta Dart,* p. 13.

26. North Korea claimed that the USS Pueblo had violated its territorial waters.

27. Marcelle Size Knaack. *Encyclopedia of US Air Force Aircraft & Missile Systems, Volume 1,* p. 217.

28. Bert Kinzey. *F-106 Delta Dart,* p. 30.

29. Some sources indicate 650 rounds of 20mm ammunition carried, the 625 rounds specification used here was obtained from a USAF Standard Aircraft Characteristics sheet.

30. Don Carson & Lou Drendel. *F-106 Delta Dart in Action,* p. 44.

31. A fourth F-106A was scheduled to take part in the exercise but was forced to abort prior to takeoff.

32. Peter Grier. *"Gary, You Better Get Back In It!",* Air Force Magazine, April 2009, p. 68-70.

33. United States Air Force Museum. *United States Air Force Museum, Aircraft Brochure,* p. 124.

34. Ray Wagner. *American Combat Planes,* p. 473.

35. These units consisted of the 101st FIS Massachusetts ANG, 119th FIS New Jersey ANG, and the 159th FIS Florida ANG.

36. *Unmanned Vehicles Forecast,* Forecast International, April 1999.

37. Iblid.

38. Iblid.

39. Dryden Flight Research Center. *Past Project – Eclipse Tow Launch Demonstration.*

40. Bert Kinzey. *F-106 Delta Dart,* p. 8.

41. Iblid, p.8.

42. National Museum of the US Air Force. *Convair F-106A Fact Sheet.*

# BIBLIOGRAPHY

Aart, Dick van der. *Aerial Espionage*, Arco Aviation Books, Simon & Schuster, New York, New York, 1986.

Anderton, David. *Republic F-105 Thunderchief*, Osprey Publishing Limited, London, 1983.

Bishop, Chris (Editor). *The Encyclopedia of 20th Century Air Warfare*, Aerospace Publishing Ltd., 2001.

Bonds, Ray (Editor). *The Vietnam War*, The Military Press, New York, New York, 1987.

Bonds, Ray (Editor). *The Modern US War Machine*, The Military Press, New York, New York, 1989.

Bowman, Martin W. *Fast Jet Fighters 1948-1978*, MBI Publishing Company, Osceola, Wisconsin, 2001.

Buttler, Tony. *American Secret Projects, Fighters & Interceptors 1945-1978*, Midland Publishing, Hinckley, England, 2007.

Cacutt, Len (Editor). *The World's Greatest Aircraft*, Exeter Books, New York, New York, 1988.

Carson, Don & Drendel, Lou. *F-106 Delta Dart in Action*, Squadron/ Signal Publications, Inc., Carrollton, Texas, 1974.

Cooper, Bryan & Batchelor, John. *Fighter*. Charles Scribner's Sons, New York, 1973.

Davis, Larry. *F-102A Delta Dart in action*, Squadron/Signal Publications, Carrollton, Texas, 2005.

Davis, Larry. *Wild Weasel*, Squadron Signal Publications, Carrollton, Texas, 1986.

Dobbs, Michael. *One Minute to Midnight*, Alfred A. Knopf, New York, New York, 2008.

Drendel, Lou. *...And Kill MiGs*, Squadron/Signal Publications, Inc., Carrollton, Texas, 1984.

Eden, Paul (Editor). *The Encyclopedia of Aircraft of WWII*, Aerospace Publishing Ltd., 2004.

Francillon, René J. *McDonnell Douglas Aircraft since 1920 Volume II*, Naval Institute Press, Annapolis, Maryland, 1990.

Friddell, Phillip. *F-104 Starfighter in Action*, Squadron Signal Publications, Carrollton, Texas, 1993.

Gardner, Thomas E. *F-100 Super Sabre at War*, Zenith Press, Minneapolis, Minnesota, 2007.

Gibson, James. *The History of the US Nuclear Arsenal*. Brompton Books Corp., Greenwich, Connecticut, 1989.

Greenhalgh, William H. *The Air Force in Southeast Asia, The RF-101 Voodoo 1961-1970*, Office of Air Force History, Washington D. C., 1979.

Green, William. *Famous Fighters of the Second World War*. Doubleday and Company, Inc., Garden City, New York, 1967.

Green, William. *The World's Fighting Planes*. Doubleday and Company, Inc., Garden City, New York, 1965.

Gunston, Bill. *American Warplanes*. Crescent Books, New York, 1986.

Gunston, Bill. *Fighters of the Fifties*. Specialty Press, Osceola, Wisconsin, 1981.

Gunston, Bill & Spick, Mike. *Modern Air Combat*. Crescent Books, New York, 1983.

Gunston, Bill. *Modern Military Aircraft*. Crescent Books, New York, 1978.

Gunston, Bill. *The Encyclopedia of World Air Power*. Crescent Books, New York, 1986.

Gunston, Bill (Editor). *The Illustrated History of Fighters*. Exeter Books, New York, 1983.

Huenecke, Klaus. *Modern Combat Aircraft Design*. The Naval Institute Press, Annapolis, Maryland, 1987.

Jones, Lloyd S. *U.S. Fighters, Army-Air Force 1925-1980s*. Aero Publishers, Fallbrook, California, 1975.

Kinzey, Burt. *F-106 Delta Dart*, Squadron/Signal Publications, Inc., Carrollton, Texas, 1983.

Knaack, Marcelle, Size. *Encyclopedia of US Air Force Aircraft & Missile Systems, Volume 1,* Office of Air Force History, Washington D. C., 1978.

March, Peter. *Sabre to Stealth, 50 Years of the United States Air Force 1947-1997.* The Royal Air Force Benevolent Fund Enterprises, *Gloucester,* England, 1997.

Mueller, Robert. *The United States Air Force Reference Series, Air Force Bases, Active Air Force Bases Within the United States.* Office of Air Force History, 1982.

Mutza, Wayne. *CONVAIR F-102 Delta Dagger,* Schiffer Publishing Ltd., Atglen, Pennsylvania, 1999.

Nalty, Bernard C. *Tactics and Techniques of Electronic Warfare, Electronic Countermeasures in the Air War Against North Vietnam 1965-1973,* Office of Air Force History, Washington D. C., 1977.

Neubeck, Ken. *F-105 Thunderchief in action,* Squadron/Signal Publications, Inc., Carrollton, Texas, 2002.

Pace, Steve. *X-Fighters.* Motorbooks International, Osceola, Wisconsin, 1991.

Price, Alfred. *Air Battle Central Europe,* The Free Press, New York, New York, 1986.

Ragay, J. D.. *F-102 Delta Dagger in Europe,* Squadron/Signal Publications Inc., Carrollton, Texas, 1991.

Robertson, Lt. Colonel Frank H.. *Military Assistance Training Program,* Air University Review, September-October 1968.

Robinson, Anthony. *Air Power – The World's Air Forces,* Orbis Publishing Ltd., London, 1980.

Taylor, John W. R. & Swanborough, Gordon. *Military Aircraft of the World.* Ian Allen, London, 1975.

Taylor, Michael J. H. & John W. R. *Missiles of the World,* Ian Allen, London, 1972.

Winchester, Jim. *American Military Aircraft.* Barnes & Noble Books, New York, 2005.

Winchester, Jim. *Fighter, The World's Finest Combat Aircraft-1914 to the Present Day.* Parragon Publishing, Bath, United Kingdom, 2004.

# INDEX

Misty forward air control operations,
34
Mitsubishi, 134
Mk.5/6 Sabre, 122
Moore, General Joseph H., 155
Mount Taylor, New Mexico, 29
Muroc Air Force Base, 38
Muroc Army Airfield, 3, 5, 142
Mystére IVA, 136-137

Naha Air Base, 87, 90
Nape, Laos, 163
National Advisory Committee for
Aeronautics (NACA), 66, 72, 91, 97,
138, 148
National Aeronautics and Space
Administration (NASA), 91, 138-
139, 201-202
National Museum of the US Air
Force, 198
North Atlantic Treaty Organization
(NATO), 24-25, 27, 36, 93, 122, 124,
126, 129, 143
Naval Ordnance Test Station, 110
Naval Weapons Center, 172
Naya Chor, Pakistan, 137
Nellis Air Force Base, 155, 161
Netherlands, 37, 86, 124, 129, 136
Nord Griffon II research aircraft, 155
North American Air Defense
Command (NORAD), 62, 190
North American Aviation, 11, 13-18,
20, 22-24, 28, 35, 40, 41, 56, 69, 96-97
North American F-100 Super Sabre,
design of, 13-14; first flight, 15;
initial operational service, 17;
stability issues, 17-19; C model, 20-
21; D model, 22-23; two-seat F
model, 23-24; service with the
Thunderbirds, 24-25; operations in
Europe, 25-27; ZEL trials, 27-28;

operations in Southeast Asia, 29-34;
Wild Weasel operations, 31-34; Air
National Guard service, 34-35;
export service, 35-37
North American Search and Ranging
Radar (NASARR), 124, 126, 130, 133
-134, 156, 169
North Vietnamese Air Force, 173
Northrop Corporation, 56, 66, 97, 140
Norway, 126, 128-129, 136
Nouasseur Air Base, 48
Nuclear Weapons,
Mk-7, 26
Mk-28 (B28), 26, 159
Mk-43 (B43), 26
Mk-57 (B57), 26
Mk-61 (B61), 26

Ohain, Hans von, 1-2
Olympus B.01.22R turbojet, 177
Ontario, California, 55
Ontario International Airport, 49
Operation Barrel Roll, 163
Operation Bell Tone, 87
Operation Candy Machine, 88, 90
Operation Flaming Dart, 30, 164
Operation Flaming Dart II, 164
Operation Julius Caesar, 24
Operation Linebacker, 176
Operation Linebacker II, 176
Operation Long Leap, 50
Operation Paperclip, 65
Operation Peach Wings, 63
Operation Rolling Thunder, 30, 118,
164, 166
Operation Sun Run, 49, 50
Operation Waterglass, 88
Orenda Engines Ltd., 131
Osan Air Base, 196
Otis Air Force Base, 58, 60

CPSIA information can be obtained at www.ICGtesting.com
Printed in the USA
LVOW121308220513

334998LV00003B/578/P